'Compelling reading.' *Monthly*

'Her vivid narrative voice lends a gritty poetry to her tale of heroin addiction, half-hearted rehab and prostitution.' *Observer*

'Verdict—better than sex.' *Canberra City News*

'An old, almost archetypal story, but it's the poignant way Holden tells it that makes it so compelling… We are enriched.' *New Review*

'Quite simply in a class of its own.' *Guardian*

'Her story resists the obvious cliches. It confounds and surprises and challenges preconceived ideas.' *Courier-Mail*

'Subtle and elegant.' *Kirkus*

'A hard book to put down.' *Advertiser*

'Confessional sex-and-redemption books are practically a dime a dozen nowadays, so it's good to be able to recommend one that is genuinely worth reading. A fresh insight into social stigma.' *New Weekly*

'Her talents as a prostitute won her a large clientele. So should her talents as a writer.' *Independent*

'Brave, explicit and extremely well written.' *ABR*

'So much more intriguing than the wastrel norm.' *Globe and Mail*

## Kate Gould

5th February 1977 – 9th October 2017

From a collection of books gathered by Kate Gould for her PhD on the ways in which media coverage of "pink Viagra" represented and constructed female sexuality; in her years at the front line of gender politics as part of the global sisterhood; and as a passionate campaigner for the truth and rights of women.

<u>Critical Sisters posted this on hearing of Kate's death:</u>

'Love and anger course through the radical feminist community compelling each of us to question, debate and create change. Many of us never met Kate in real life, and yet she spoke our truth often in the face of hostility. Her clear and unwavering voice rang out through her writing - righteous, powerful and insightful. Without ego and free from artifice - Kate's bravery, shining intellect and warmth have inspired many of us. Kate gave to each of us; and her memory and work continue to give us strength. We will miss our sister.'

**ALSO BY THE AUTHOR**

*In My Skin: a memoir*

Kate Holden's first book, the bestselling *In My Skin: a memoir*, was published by Text in 2005 to critical acclaim and released in eleven other countries. Kate has also written a popular column for Melbourne's *Age* newspaper for several years, as well as widely published essays, short stories and literary criticism. After time in Rome, Shanghai and London, she once more lives in Melbourne.

# THE ROMANTIC

## ITALIAN NIGHTS AND DAYS

KATE
HOLDEN

TEXT PUBLISHING MELBOURNE AUSTRALIA

The paper used in this book is manufactured only from wood grown in sustainable regrowth forests.

The Text Publishing Company
Swann House
22 William Street
Melbourne Victoria 3000
Australia
textpublishing.com.au

'Black Coffee' by J Burke and Paul Webster © Copyright Sondot Music Corp/Criterion Music Corp administered by Origin Music Publishing Pty Ltd
All print rights for Origin Music Publishing Pty Ltd administered in Australia and New Zealand by Sasha Music Publishing, a division of All Music Publishing & Distribution Pty Ltd
ACN 079 628 434 ABN 79 079 628 434
PO Box 1031 Richmond North Victoria 3121 Australia
www.ampd.com.au
Used By Permission. All Rights Reserved. Unauthorised Reproduction is Illegal.

'Black Coffee' Words and music by Paul Webster/Francis Burke © Webster Music Co. administered in Australia/New Zealand by Rondor Music Australia Pty. Ltd.
All rights reserved. International copyright secured. Reprinted with permission.

Every effort has been made to trace copyright holders and obtain permission for the use of copyright material. The publisher apologises for any errors or omissions and would be grateful if notified of any corrections that should be incorporated in future reprints or editions of this book.

First published by The Text Publishing Company, 2010

Cover design by WH Chong
Page design by Susan Miller
Typeset by J&M Typesetting

National Library of Australia
Cataloguing-in-Publication entry

Holden, Kate, 1972-

The romantic / Kate Holden.

ISBN: 9781921656743 (pbk.)

Subjects: Holden, Kate, 1972-
Relationship addiction—Australia—Biography.
Love

306.7092

 This project has been assisted by the Commonwealth Government through the Australia Council, its arts funding and advisory body.

To those who have taught me best
and those who love me now.

And to Pete (1971-2010), who
started me with sweetness.

This is a work of imagination as well
as truth. All names have been changed
and characterisation compressed. It is
a sincere memory in shaped retrospect.
The author is real.

part one

# JACK

*Man's love is of man's life a thing apart;*
*'Tis woman's whole existence.*
**BYRON**

'Are you still coming?'

'Should I?'

The sound of his amusement. 'Only if you want to.'

'But only if you want me to. I don't want to impose.' She stifles pleasure. 'I'd hate to ruin your peace and quiet.'

'Ruin it. I want to see you.'

She hesitates, then, 'I'm on my way. I'm on my way. I'll be on the train that gets in at six-fifteen. Look out for a small but extremely sexy girl with a big smile.'

'Woman. Not girl.'

'This *woman* will be very happy to see you tonight.'

Jack invites, and she goes. Should she have hesitated instead, for form's sake? Don't women say you should make men chase you? She'd said yes to his invitation, that night at the pub in Rome, after they'd kissed, almost before he'd finished asking. And then blushed. 'I won't be in the way,' she'd added. She wondered why she was letting him take the lead. The whole thing was probably a whim of his, wouldn't last. But he'd breathed into her breasts that first night, and said, 'I need this. God, I didn't realise how much. Kate. You're *lovely*.' And he had that sexy mouth. She had enjoyed making him smile again and again.

Six hours south on the train from Rome. Her palms are damp. She is aware that in a way this is the best part: the anticipation. Tonight she will be fucking. Her slack body will twist and surge. She imagines it, and her cheek grows hot against the cold train window. In the minutes before the train pulls in, she finds that she feels nothing, after all.

But when she climbs down onto the platform she forgets to smile neatly: her mouth opens helplessly in delight. She walks towards him through the crowd, careful to look casual, but she is wearing lipstick, and she is half his age.

'It's very good to see you.' And there is his grin.

His mouth is shockingly warm against hers in the safety of the car.

✦

She has come to Italy in search of three things: Rome, Romantics and Romance. Four things. Herself.

Rome seems the best place. She had to leave Australia. And here, in the city of eternity, she might find something to help her endure. She can lose herself, before she is found.

Nothing to do but explore. Nothing to be but a ghost. It is freedom, at last.

Money saved to live on; a friend of a friend with a spare room in his apartment; the months ahead. This city she has dreamed of, sunlight at the end of a tunnel.

In her notebook, the motto that Shelley had inscribed on a ring when he arrived in Italy: *Il buon tempo verrà*. The good time is coming.

And so she comes to Rome, and arrives on a gilded autumn day. She looks out at the kindness of sunlight on the buildings; the warm sky cupped like a hand above her head, the milky air, and hopes that here she will find gentleness.

The lies of the past few years have made her skin clammy, softened her bones until she barely knows her own shape. Now her task is that of the Romantics she loves so much: to realise herself, to become her true self. She knows it won't be easy. *To be abused for having a human heart is common but always cruel,* she writes in her diary.

Italy will be a test. It will clarify. It will precipitate. She wants peace, she wants understanding, after the years in darkness she wants to become, finally, a woman who is bright and clear.

✦

His house is in a sea of olive trees. They bend their grey leaves around silvery light; they spread around the cottage like a frisky ocean. Beyond, a pale line, is the sea itself. She and Jack stand on the flat roof, looking out on the morning mild as a dream. 'You live in a tower at the end of the world,' she says. 'You remind me of a prince in a fairy story, who withdraws from the world to meditate on a magic mirror. Or his collection of broken clocks.'

'Alas. This prince has to go to work. Will you be all right?'

'I'll be fine.' She turns and wraps herself around him. His mouth is crisp and rather thin, an Englishman's mouth all right. His lips are a little dry. But his tongue is as wet as any young man's. She thinks of the picture they must make, two figures entwined on a rooftop, the only vertical things above this silvery sea. And even they might topple, under the drag of this want. 'I'll be waiting for you.'

He gazes at her. Those blue impertinent eyes. 'It's good to see you. Thank you for coming down. I enjoy your company.'

She laughs, because he means so many more things. 'It's good to be seen. Now off you go. I'll be reading poetry all day and looking nymph-like.'

'God help me,' he says, kisses her one more time and walks

down the stairs. She pauses, but hurries after him for another last kiss.

✦

The day is cool but she takes a plate of salami and cheese back up to the rooftop, settles on the ground against the low parapet, and opens her Byron.

> The whisper'd thought of hearts allied,
> The pressure of the thrilling hand...

She puts the lines aside.

So far, so good. He seems pleased, more than pleased, to see her. They have established a little routine, all in one night: he is the rueful older man, she the provocative sprite. He shakes his head as he takes off her silver rings before they make love; she watches, delighted to have a man do such a thing so tenderly.

'Silver is for teenagers,' he says. 'You should have just a nice simple gold ring.'

'Is that a proposal?' It could never be any such thing, not after one night, not even if he said this in a year's time. For one thing, there's a wife somewhere. Anyway, she loves her silver rings.

He laughs. 'Don't push it.' And kisses her, pulls her down onto the rug by the fire in a lounge room in the south of Italy with glasses of local wine on the hearth—O, *for a beakerful of the warm South!* They make love and she feels so powerful then, because she can make him moan, while all the time she has her eyes open and can watch him be undone by her.

It is his turn to watch, though, as they untangle themselves afterwards. 'You're almost too good at this.'

She looks at him, suddenly wary. 'I like men. I like making them happy.'

6

He says nothing more, but fetches wine.

He has already noticed that there's something wrong with her. He says, after the third glass, 'There's something in your face...'

'What?'

'You have a lovely face.' She blushes. 'But something... You're not quite formed yet. And you're what? Thirty? You haven't arrived. When you look soft you're just lovely. You almost look like a child.'

'I promise you, I'm a haggard old woman inside.'

'Oh, I don't think so. No, you're a sumptuous young lady with, I must say, gorgeous breasts. It's I who's the ancient ruin. You'll be sorry in a day or two, to have got stuck with me.'

She runs her hand up his thigh, holds his penis. 'You do pretty well, old man. I think we're good at this.' She looks up at him, tender. The wine has blurred his mouth. 'It's so nice to find someone who's like me.'

'Yes.' He takes her hand away from his cock, holds her fingers. 'I think we are alike.'

The two of them, a married man and a woman half his age, sit by the fire and whisper secrets. *I love being on my own. Other people tire me. When I get by myself, it's like a door slamming, all my shutters come down, I'm not so sure that's a good thing. Oh, I know what you mean. I'm like that. Maybe I'm happiest on my own. Yes, me too. But then...it's nice to be with someone, the right someone. You're lovely. You're lovely. Come here.*

*Now don't fall in love with me, will you.*

*God, no!*

And they laugh.

On the rooftop, she thinks of him coming, how harshly he'd breathed, his body tensed as he'd said, Oh Kate, oh Kate I'm going to come, and his clipped English voice had broken.

She remembers this and the blood prickles on her scalp. She didn't come, but next time, maybe, soon.

This is an adventure—it's what she came here for. There *was* something missing in her; she'd been told so before, felt it in herself. A kind of passivity. She didn't take anything seriously: it wasn't real. This blankness gave her courage. If nothing mattered, then nothing could hurt. Perhaps she needs something to hurt, to make it all real.

✦

They move closer, ever closer. He is at work all day; she reads Byron, writes her journal, tidies the house, and then, before he comes home, she washes, dresses, places candles on the steps of the stairs to welcome him, waits. There is pleasure in the ritual of preparation; she wants everything to be perfect; her heart beats high in her chest as she hears the car door slam. She is a little sheepish at the display she makes: is it too much, will he see she is sentimental? A delicate balance between pleasing and foolishness. But when he walks into the room to find the fire lit, the bottle of wine standing, the girl opening her arms and twining herself around him, he pulls back to smile at her and say, 'Thank you. This is wonderful. Oh, it's glorious to come home to you.'

She eases: this pleasure is allowed. She is a good house guest, she rewards her host. Making him laugh is her success; making him come is her currency. They are growing more knitted, more intimate. How he loves to talk to her. This impetus, this drawing out of their damp, fragile secrets and doubts. And she reveals herself—though not everything, because some things are best left unmentioned. She doesn't talk about the past. She doesn't tell him that the sex that so electrified her has become a little dull as he seems to be growing tired. Their tussle on the fireplace rug grows shorter every night: more of a prelude to the talk. But he stands in front of her and brings his lips to within an inch of hers, and then waits, smiling; shivers of desire pass up and down her, and at those moments it is he who watches her, helpless and overcome.

As they make love in the early light he says, 'Are you afraid I'll fall in love with you?'

She looks at him straight. 'Yes. A bit. I mean, I want you to like me…'

'I'm very fond of your company.' He loves being English, so restrained. She nips his ear, she gets the joke. 'But as for falling…'

'It's just that—I don't think you will, but—if you did, I mightn't be able to take you seriously anymore. I always find that when someone falls for me, I seem to lose respect for them. I think there must be something wrong with them.' She slithers down to kiss his nipples.

'There's nothing wrong with me. And I promise I shan't fall in love with you.'

'Good,' she says through a mouthful of cock.

It's almost too easy, to play his body. To know how to press, stroke, cajole, grip and tense against him so that he'll gasp— so—and buck—so. She's perversely impressed when, despite her ministrations and caresses, his cock that morning fails to rise. Ah. Resistance. So she won't start to despise him, after all.

He leaves for work and she pleasures herself, so intently and deliberately it's almost vicious.

✦

The horizon ebbs and nears throughout the day. Up on the parapet she looks across the silver olives, to the rim of sea, and beyond to a winter sky that gleams, light on metal. The three elements merge. Sometimes the sea appears close; other days it has melted into the sky. She stands over it all in her black clothes: a breach in the easy blue, or something whole?

At night as she puts the candles out for Jack's homecoming she pauses and looks out to the darkness. She has never lived anywhere as far away as this: far from other people, far from lights. Just her, one human in all the emptiness. Out there the olive trees crouch, baskets of black air. She feels the wind that has run through the trees to rush her skin. She is part of something here; she stands as still as an olive tree, hoping for such endurance.

Planted in the soil of Jack's attention, she feels immensely grateful; has been adrift here in Italy in this short time, alone in Rome: blundering around city streets, endlessly walking to no destination, no precious contact with another human, a mere sightseer. There is no internet in the flat where she lives nor anywhere close, no landline; phone calls are so expensive; the world she has left recedes past reach. It is what she wanted, to get away; but she had grown lonely. Here she has found one who cares about her.

Though she stares at him as he sleeps; she knows, but it prickles, that she might be playing a little game. When all she wants is sincerity. She forces herself to recognise it: the fear in herself that she is not the admirable girl he thinks she is; the times she's felt one thing and put another on her face. The comfort of pushing him away, though he never knows it, with her cool scientific stare.

All this time alone, in the peace of the olive field. It is unsettling.

✦

The next morning she wakes up unhappy. Contentment has rinsed off her like soap. It's gone. She is alarmed, naked. Nothing has happened; it is only that everything amazes her with its pointlessness. She stares at the kettle in Jack's kitchen with a kind of fright. How, she thinks, have I come to be here, in this room, holding this kettle bought by a man I don't know—this Jack—oh god, what does he see: some awful girl, with all her tricks and contrivances, *this fucking head of hers*? She goes to the bathroom mirror. What looks back is tired and ugly and uneasy.

The afternoon hours before he gets home are the slowest. Up to the rooftop, to look at the view; but the olive trees are a dirty green, the sea she might visit is too far away, she'd have to walk through the fields, the farmer might see her, she could get lost, what if it were hours away, how would she get home? The sea is the only thing in sight, there is nowhere else. Shelley has understood this unhappiness:

> The lightning of the noontide ocean
> Is flashing round me, and a tone
> Arises from its measured motion,
> How sweet! did any heart now share in my emotion.
>
> Alas! I have nor hope nor health,
> Nor peace within nor calm around,
>
> …Nor fame nor power, nor love, nor leisure,
> Others I see whom these surround -
> Smiling they live, and call life pleasure; -
> To me that cup has been dealt in another measure…

She's trapped here on this turret, some kind of Rapunzel. She fingers her short hair. 'You'd look lovely with long hair,' he'd said. 'It's more feminine.' But she'd cut off her long hair when she arrived in Italy, to feel more definite. 'You let yourself behave like a child,' he says. 'That won't get you anywhere. You're an adult, you're a fine grown woman, stop pretending you're not. You do yourself a disservice.'

'I like my hair like this.'

'Why don't you try it long? And get rid of those ridiculous rings while you're about it.' He is teasing her, his eyes bright with enjoyment. 'Stop being a child.'

She can't. Perhaps he's right, she's backwards. She doesn't know how to do it any other way; doesn't like gold. He's put his finger on it: there's something slack in her, some kind of disability. She is nearly thirty and she's dressing like a student ten years younger. Harking back to the last time she knew who she was and felt strong. Today she feels weak and lost; the air pressure in her is too low.

She stands at the parapet and smokes and smokes to fill herself.

And when Jack gets home he finds the living room dark and candlelit, with her standing quiet. She raises her face stricken and stilled—perhaps just a little bit in her is making a spectacle out of this, because she can't risk that he won't notice. Her heart pounds with misery. He steps back. 'Jesus Christ,' he says, 'who died?' And flips on the light.

The glow of the candle flames vanishes in the bright room. 'You look a sight,' he says. She comes forward and embraces him, still not speaking, pressing her unhappiness against his solidity. 'For god's sake.'

He kisses her swiftly and moves to the other side of the room, wrenching his name tag off his jacket. 'I guess you've been reading that bloody misery poetry all afternoon while some of us have been out making the world work. Well, come on, let's get the fire going and make some dinner. It's been a hell of a day.'

And she forces a smile and says, 'Tell me all about it, my dear.'

Later, she tries to explain her sadness. Mild, in the firelight, cupping her wine, not looking at him. It's hard, after a lifetime of not showing it, to reveal this uncertainty, to trust him. Trying to describe alarm with no cause, sorrow without a centre. She looks at him, holding back tears, hoping he'll put his arms around her and tell her what to do.

'You're indulging yourself,' he says.

She lights a cigarette to cover the shock.

'It's no good letting yourself wallow in all this. What a performance. I tell you,' he says, easing back in the chair, 'I nearly died when I walked into the room. Your face—all the candles! Such a picture of misery.'

'I was miserable. I am miserable.'

'It was an act. Come on. You're stronger than that. You were playing up to me, so I'd look after you, and be all, "Oh Kate, do tell me what's wrong."' He looks straight at her. 'That won't work with me. I don't play games. I like you very much. But you're hard work, Kate.'

'Don't be cruel,' she says, pulling her knees up to her chin.

'I'm not being cruel, I'm being honest. Don't hunch up like a child, sit up tall and proud. Listen. I don't need hard work. I'm an old man who likes his peace and quiet. What you have to do is work to your strengths. That's what I do. I've been the good guy all my life, I've done what I had to to get myself a quiet life. My wife is back home; I am here. Sometimes I'm lonely and I feel sorry for myself, and sometimes I understand that you have to just resist that kind of thinking. It's your life, and you have to decide how you'll live it. And I can tell you that skulking in a dark room reading poetry won't work. Be yourself, be the wonderful young woman I like so much.' He holds out his hand.

She takes it. Pushes down her hurt. Indulging herself; yes, she'd indulged the sweet pain. His hand is strong and dry. She kisses the knuckles, waiting to know what to say. 'It's easy for you. You have a life, a job, a wife. I don't have anything.'

He sighs. 'You're not listening. You'll be fine. After all, here I am, a foolish old man, and I'm okay. I have some wisdom, so let me share it with you. Life is a game and you have to play it right.'

'I thought you said you don't play games.'

'Not stupid emotional games, no.'

'What about this with me?'

'I'm not playing a game with you.' He bends forward, brings his face near to hers. There is that ripple through her, as she looks at his mouth so close. 'I'm trying to help you.'

'Help me, then,' she says, defeated, 'by taking my clothes off.'

✣

The next day she wakes resolved to heed his advice. Rinse off the clammy sadness. She cleans the house, stacks the firewood, walks among the olive trees in the sunshine, and waits for him with a cheery smile. He says, 'Here, I bought you something,' and hands over a book. Byron's *Selected Poems*. He winks at her. 'But no skulking.'

It is kindness, it is a reward.

✣

The next evening he catches her hand. He takes it in hers as they walk through the olives in the winter sunset, ducking their heads under the gnarled branches, admiring the twisted, timeless trunks.

'You're so lucky to live here,' she says.

'Am I? I like it. It's not so convenient; all the other chaps live in town near the office. But I've always loved the country. Our house back home is country. We even have chickens.'

'Do you rake the chicken shit?' She pictures him, gumboots on, flannel shirt, sturdy hoe, man of the land. Fastidious Jack. It makes her laugh.

'Heroically. Night and day. You wouldn't believe how much those birds can make.'

'Do you miss it?'

He hesitates. 'I love the place. We have three fields, horses, a cottage garden. The whole disaster.'

'Very English.'

'It's tranquil. Maybe too much. I sometimes think that's what I want, but when I go back there on leave, after a couple of weeks I can't escape fast enough.' He raises a hand, places it on a bough over his head. 'I'm hard to satisfy.'

'You don't seem too hard to satisfy. Last night,' she says, leadingly. The way lovers celebrate their love, mumble it over and over, reminiscing almost before each joy is over. Or is it just her? Jack will probably resist this sentimentality.

'I remember.' No, he won't resist. He has the same secret curl to his lips.

'We're good together.' Even though she can't come with him. It doesn't matter.

'Yes. Though there's—'

'What?'

'There's something about how good we are. Almost too good.' So he hasn't forgotten that he already said this. That she distracted him. She can see it in his eyes: he's wondering what he has been deceived about.

'You're right. Yeah. There's this thing.' She too puts her hand on the branch; studies it. After all the times she's practised to herself, she can't meet his eyes. 'I should have told you. But I thought you'd—anyway. I should have told you.' Here we go: give away the game. No. We don't play games.

He waits.

'I think you'll understand. You understand that people have long lives, interesting lives. They do all sorts of things. Think of all the things *you've* done. People do good things and bad things, they seem a good idea at the time, it's how we learn...' She's dithering. But best to prepare, to anticipate, to weave protection before the exposure. Or *disclosure*. There's a term for it. It sounds like the opposite of closure; unfair, when she is so certain it is all behind her.

'I was a heroin addict,' she says. The words still sound so stupid, so formal. Like a euphemism. Jack loves those. 'I did heroin for five years. I also worked as a prostitute.' A harder word. A harsh word that she insists on using.

Keep going. 'On the street. Then in brothels.' *Brothel.* All these ugly words. And no time, she knows already, to describe that it wasn't all ugly, that some of it was beautiful. But how sordid it sounds, told like this. She remembers the glamorous light, the rancid sweat, the cosmetics and the red velvet gown, the laughter and the utter exhaustion. Jack won't want to hear that. He won't want to hear that she is proud of it.

She looks at him, biting her lip.

'I thought so.'

'What?'

'I thought that might be it. You're too good, that's what I said.' He almost looks pleased, to have been correct. 'So that's why you're here?'

She doesn't know if he means Italy, or here with him. 'Yes.'

'That's what's in your face,' he says. 'I catch glimpses sometimes.'

She puts a hand over her mouth. 'Do you?' Makes herself take her hand away. 'I wasn't a bad person. It was a time in my life. It's over now. I'm here to get away from all that.'

He says nothing, then, only takes his hand from the branch and turns to head back to the house. She pulls her own hand from the bark slowly, so it scrapes, and follows.

✦

And when they make love, she wonders if he's watching her for the signs of artifice, that she's an expert whore; when she slides down to take him in her mouth she blushes. Slides up again and kisses him. Sets herself: don't apologise. It's hard, but she mustn't. She's not going to give up sex, just because she's had sex before, because she's *too good* at it. Sex isn't about being good. Sex is between people. With others, she might mangle her kisses. With Jack, she is good.

But she begins to watch herself now, to see how automatically she moves from one position to another; when she places her ankles on his shoulders his look of surprise; she hears herself breathing dramatically and wonders if it's habit. She can't tell. She can't actually tell.

She rolls away, gets on top, rears upright. She puts a finger on herself, massages, licks it and puts it back there. This is the test, this is how she recovers. She fights her body, fights to disregard Jack's hot perplexed gaze, to find the lines of tension in herself and pull them together: gasping, she yanks the lines through her body like threads of fire.

Jack says afterwards, 'My last lover could come in a few minutes. It's harder with you.'

She thinks, Maybe she was a better whore. She says, rolling her eyes, 'Oh, you men. It's too bad we're so tricky.'

She thinks, Did I expect it to be fair?

Now the questions begin: how did you feel when an ugly man came to the brothel? Did you ever come? Did the other girls? Didn't you despise them, those lonely men? What kinds of things did they want? Wasn't it all ghastly? How did you—what, so you had to make the bed after each client? You can make the beds here, then. What was Greek? Oh. Why were the other women doing the job, if they weren't all on drugs? Tell me more. Tell me…

'Do you really want to hear this?' she says, disbelieving.

'It's fascinating. I've never been to a prostitute. Never had the need. What was the worst client you had?'

She lets it go now, the torrents of information she's been keeping to herself for months. All the stuff she *knows*, that others don't know. She explains, analyses, talks about the economics and the sexual politics and the socio-geographic aspects and what a golden shower is and how the rubbish bin full of condoms stank so bad at the end of each night and how the lonely men nearly broke her heart. She tells it, relieved. He is the first person she's really told it to.

And he keeps asking, listening, laughing too. It was that easy, after all.

+

But he is exhausted after a week of late nights and company. 'I told you. I'm just a curmudgeon.'

'Oh my poor handsome curmudgeon. My poor broken man. Shall we have an early night?'

'Actually, I was thinking…' He puts his arms loosely around her waist. 'Perhaps I should sleep alone tonight. You can sleep in the spare room. There's a bed all made up for when I have visitors. Which I never do.'

She doesn't know what he is saying. 'Of course. You need a good sleep. That's fine.'

'I think, actually, that we shouldn't have sex anymore.'

'Oh.'

'I wonder if I gave you the wrong impression. I very much enjoy fucking you, Kate. Perhaps too much. But…I don't seem to be able to keep up the pace.' He is embarrassed, she is wise enough to see that. 'In some ways I wish we'd never—that we'd just talked, instead. I do like talking with you. But I worry that I'm going to disappoint you, and also…I think I might be compromising myself. My wife…We don't go to bed anymore, I told you that. But I think I'd rather keep this special with you, and not ruin things. Maybe on the weekend. I *am* tired.'

She observes him. Could it be—it can't be—because of what she told him? Well, here it is. She is ready, she realises, for the injury. Already the smooth carapace of sympathy and understanding is setting on her face. She'll make the flattering noises as well. 'Oh, but I love fucking you.' She runs her hand over his groin. 'Are you sure? Well, okay. Maybe you're right.' Chagrin at the rejection; reprieve, at no longer having to fear herself, the sexy doll she becomes in bed.

'It'll make you feel better, too. Not to be so wanton.'

'Hah, hah.'

That night they say a courteous goodnight; he gives her a long, considering look that makes her want to push him onto the bed; she says, 'Well, sweet dreams.' She knows that she is proving herself with this; it isn't a loss. She'll play the game.

✦

Without sex, they can grow closer. They relish the push and give. He says that she relies on an appearance of vulnerability to get people to look after her; she protests that she wants only to be strong. He accuses her of manipulation; she admits it. 'I don't want to, with you, though. I want to be honest. I want you to see the real me.'

He says her clothes are barbaric. 'You hunch. You whisper. It's excruciating to see. You have to take possession of yourself. How often do I have to reassure you: you're an extraordinary woman. Be it.'

'I know I…but I'm just not a bold outspoken person. I'm polite. I don't like brashness.'

'Stop being so self-conscious.'

'How can I be, how can I consciously try not to be self-conscious? It's impossible!' She is laughing.

'Just be yourself. My god, how hard can that be?'

But it is the hardest thing. She knows that she is trying to please him. So can she ever find out her real self while playing the version he wants her to be?

In turn, she accuses him of being a faker. Of engineering a genteel personality, responsible and restrained, when inside she has seen a glint of the wicked boy. 'Oh poor man,' she says. 'How you hold yourself back.'

'I don't, with you. I let myself be exactly who I am.'

'You don't. You're always using euphemisms. Life is for living, Jack: dare a little. Be passionate. Stop worrying all the time what the farmer next door will think; what the blokes at work think. It might do your reputation good if people know you have an incredibly gorgeous mistress at home.'

A scoffing laugh, pleased. 'Well, that might be. But I've been careful all my life, to get what I have now, and I don't intend to lose it.'

'And yet you want me to give up who I am.'

'Because you're not finished yet. I am. I'm complete. Never apologise, never look back.'

She looks at him in pity. 'You complain of being lonely.'

A sigh of acknowledgement. 'Touché.' He touches her hand. 'I'm glad you're here. Don't listen to me when I complain. I'm just *indulging*—' the word has become a running joke—'I'm just indulging myself when I say that. I'm okay on my own. Really, I am.' But she sees that he's offering her a different message with his eyes. 'Stop analysing everything. It'll drive you mad.'

'I like analysing you. There's no one,' she assures him, 'that I'd rather analyse.'

'Well. I don't know if that's a compliment.'

'It is.' She perseveres. 'You don't want to think or feel too much. You're afraid of it.' He levels his gaze at her across the rim of his glass but says nothing. 'Don't you believe in romance? In romanticism? The world is so subtle and rapturous. Poetry is full of that mystery, that's why I love it. It helps me *feel*, when most of the time I don't feel anything at all. And if I didn't try to feel, then—I'd end up like you. Hidden. It's sad.'

'Don't waste your sympathy on me,' he says. 'I don't need it. I'm fine.'

She shakes her head. 'Jack, Jack. You'll wake up when you're seventy and realise that you missed some wonderful chances. The fullness of life. Adventures. A girl who wants to make love to you, for one thing.'

'Ah, that. Yes. Well, romance isn't my thing but at least I know how to fuck.'

They exchange looks, daring the other to say, *But we don't. Fuck.*

'I don't know why I put up with this,' he says, and abruptly makes a grab with his fingers for her ribs, and tickles her until she yelps like a child.

'See? This is how you get out of conversations you don't like,' she pants. 'Scaredy-cat. You hide all your feelings, you do.'

21

'Oh Kate,' he says mockingly as they kiss goodnight later, 'I love you so much. I'm so in love with you. How's that for hiding my feelings?' He grins at her, not kindly, and turns away.

✦

'And then there's respect. I think there are two types of respect: the kind that makes you give way, you know, give a wide berth to someone, out of respect for their difference. And then there's the kind where you respect someone enough, their strength, to have a go at them, give them the credit that they can defend themselves. And perhaps you'll take something from that, or you won't. But respect, for yourself, and then for others; I think respect is the most important thing.'

He sips wine, says nothing, just watches her working out the most obvious things in the world.

✦

Now, '*You're* hard work,' she tells him. She sees it in his eyes: something fugitive, something flinching and yet hovering close behind his gaze. He won't relax, won't give in to the real pleasure possible in their relationship. He talks of 'enjoying her company' but she sees desire in his body, how he still stands close to her, how the blood flushes the base of his throat.

One night they drink more wine than usual and he becomes foolish, groping for words to explain himself. He speaks of how he'd like to go on a walking tour, just alone ('or,' he says shyly, 'perhaps with you'); he talks of the games he's had to play, his difficult marriage, the sacrifices he's made. She listens, the model of the understanding mistress. It is glorious.

They go to his bed. She holds his head between her palms, looking down on his face, how the lines smooth out, how bashfully his mouth curves in a smile below his closed eyes. He is beautiful in his shyness. And something tells her that this is as close as she will get to his truth.

So it is. He gets up in the morning, dresses briskly, and wishes her a good day. Don't, she thinks.

'Try not to skulk,' he says.

She sits up in bed. 'Have fun at work,' she says coldly, and goes back to sleep.

✦

'So. What are your plans from here?' he says that night.

She pauses in the middle of placing her dinner plate on the table. He seats himself and picks up his fork, busies himself with food.

'I was thinking,' she says, 'of going to Naples.' It comes off the top of her head. How terrible if she hadn't had an answer. She tries to ignore how sick she feels.

'Good god, why? Naples is a terrible place.'

'Have you been there?'

'For a day. I couldn't get out fast enough. Full of drug addicts and thieves. It's filthy.'

She raises an eyebrow at his disdain for addicts. 'I like the idea of it. I know it's dangerous. I think it'll be good for me. You're always telling me I should test myself. Well, I'll see how I do.'

He shakes his head, and puts more salt on his food. 'I should have known you'd say that. Well, I can't tell you what to do. I'm not your father. But I wouldn't go there if I were you. Try north, somewhere nice like Tuscany.'

She eats, upset. So he's booting her out? *Tuscany*, like she's some tourist looking for prettiness. *Nice*. He doesn't even have the guts to tell her he needs space. So English. 'But I'll come back for New Year's, in a few weeks. Like you said.'

He swallows a mouthful. 'You might get a better offer. More exciting places to be than in the middle of nowhere with an old curmudgeon.'

It's pitiful, his insecurity. Relenting, she says, 'I want to be here. With you.'

'You'll never learn,' he says, and keeps eating as she stares at him.

✦

'*Why* do you do this? Why won't you let yourself enjoy this?' She shakes his arm, half-laughing, half-furious. 'You're impossible.'

He's been telling her why it's best she leaves ('though of course you're welcome here any time'). The neighbours are giving him funny looks, he says, and he's finding it hard to concentrate at work, being so tired. He'll be going home to England for Christmas. He mentions his wife more often—not as the termagant of the first days but as someone he cares deeply about. He doesn't want to distress her. He can't risk upsetting his family. And anyway, he's just a ridiculous old man, and surely she'll be better off without him for a while. 'Go out, test yourself,' he says, as if it was his idea. 'You can't skulk around here forever, reading your bloody books.'

'Thank you for having me,' she says, deadpan.

'Well, you got some free accommodation and board out of it,' he says, as a joke.

She walks out of the room. 'I'll pay you back,' she says, loud enough for him to hear.

✦

In the car on the way to the supermarket he admits he was intimidated by her in bed. She sits there, surprised and pleased;

how tender she feels towards him for saying it. 'I didn't want you to feel that,' she says gently.

'I know. It's my problem. You were wonderful. I'm sorry, I know you were disappointed.'

'I just wanted you to feel nice.'

He keeps his eyes on the road. He is a responsible driver. 'You did. Maybe we'll get better at it.'

She wonders whether that would happen if he were no longer intimidated, if he felt he had the upper hand. She must have disturbed his equanimity. Oh, it's so boring having to take care of men's egos. But she says only, 'You know I love being in bed with you.'

They shop; she feels a little pointless, as she won't be here to eat this food. At the register he gets flustered when the check-out woman speaks to him in Italian; after three years here he knows hardly a word of it. 'She asked if you want a bag,' she says helpfully. 'Yes, of course I want a bloody bag,' he snaps at the woman, and she is embarrassed for him, this foreigner fumbling with his packet of toilet paper. There is a peculiar cruelty to sudden pity for someone you admire.

On the way home he is grim. He barely responds to her chatter, which grows more vacuous the more nervous she gets. She knows he can hardly bear her presence right now but they're twenty minutes from home, what can she do? She begins to talk about politics, the tension between pleasing the mass and considering the minority, about how it exemplifies the tension between self and other, just as in relationships, how to bestow without losing, how to fulfil without forfeit…

'God, you just never bloody stop, do you,' he says.

She pretends he's just bantering. 'Nope. I love thinking.'

'I can't be bothered thinking anymore. I learned how not to.' His hands on the steering wheel are dry and cold-looking.

'One day you'll find it's much easier.' The knuckles are reddened. There is a big vein running across one. He presses his lips together and glares at the road ahead.

'Let me tell you a funny story from the brothel, then,' she says, relentless. In a way she's enjoying his discomfort. 'There was a little Vietnamese girl I worked with, she was beautiful, just exquisite but minuscule, and then one day a guy asked her to vomit on him, just a little puke—'

'I don't want to hear any more of your stories. To be honest, suddenly I'm finding them quite revolting.'

She shuts up.

At home, they make an effort to repair the crack; he manages a smile. She goes to her room to pack her bag. When she returns to the living room he is sitting at the table, doing paperwork. She goes up to him and kisses the back of his shoulder. 'Would you like a cup of tea?'

He doesn't turn, but says, 'Can I trust an Australian heathen to make a proper cup?'

'Oh, the little colonial maid. Yes, I can make a proper cup of tea.'

She makes it. 'Your tea, milord.'

'Thank you.'

'I was just in the kitchen, being amused at myself. God, if my mother could see me. Making tea for my man. It's disgusting, really. But part of me,' she says, willing him to understand that she is mocking herself, so he doesn't have to, 'really likes being domestic. It's soothing. I even like doing the washing up.'

He makes a note on a document, smiling. 'I might keep you on, then.'

But she's leaving tomorrow. Because he asked her to.

'"I was never kinder to the old man than during the whole

week before I killed him,"' she quotes, feeling clever, and goes out to smoke a cigarette on the rooftop for the last time. Last time for now. And one last fire in the fireplace. She is conscious of her departure; she keeps looking at him, to fix him in her mind. After they've eaten he sits in his chair as usual, while she curls in front of the grate. They look at each other.

'Here's to the last two weeks,' she says, raising her glass.

'Here's to mutual misunderstandings,' he answers, grinning. 'Nice to share.'

She puts her hand on his knee, then rests her head there, silent.

'Your face is very soft,' he says. 'Lift it. Just like that. Yes, very soft. You look lovely like that.'

She looks back at him, calm. Her cheeks are warm from the fire.

'I'll miss you,' he says. 'I enjoy your company. You've been very nice to come home to. Most of the time.' There is that grin; now he's mocking himself. 'I hope I haven't been too hard to live with.'

She sighs. 'It's been wonderful.' The sea of olives, the crisp air, the silence. Reading poetry in a shaft of sunshine amid shadows. Fetching wood for the fire. Lighting the candles to guide him up the stairs every night. This fire, this wine, this man: this image of safety. Tears well in her eyes, but she remembers she mustn't be sentimental.

'You'll be my last lover, you know.'

'Oh yes?'

'I've trusted you. Yes. You'll be the last.'

'I don't believe you.' She stirs, gets to her feet. 'Come outside with me. Let's go and get some air.'

'But it's freezing out there. Why do you want to go out into the dark?'

27

'It's my last night. Come on. It'll be good for you.'

They walk out of the farmhouse and into the great darkness. The olive trees are motionless. But there is the full moon, and the world, once her eyes adjust, lit with its white stare. A glass bowl of silence surrounds them.

'You and your barbaric clothes,' he says, looking at her swathed in black scarves.

'Shut up. You love them,' she takes his hand.

'Oh Kate. I do love you dearly. Whatever am I going to do without you?' Their hands clamped together for warmth.

'Shhh,' she says, and kisses him. How hot his mouth is.

They break the kiss and look out at the road ahead, embarrassed. 'I'll catch a cold.'

'But look. Look.'

The road has become a river of light. On either side the olive trees make eldritch shapes, their buckled branches black and the leaves white. She sees the shadows: how light makes its own fugitives. The glowing path disappears around a bend; she takes a few steps forwards. 'It's like a road going to another world,' she whispers. 'It's here, all the time.'

He clenches her hand. 'You and your imagination. Bloody hell.' He kisses her on the forehead. 'Come on inside.'

They go back to the house, but she casts a glance behind.

✦

On the train to Naples she smells like sex. They didn't make love one last time. Too much caution—caution inside, the kind you coddle, telling yourself it's safety. They kissed though, they kissed passionately and she finds that even the next day her body is saturated with arousal. She smells just like a woman loved.

The train takes her back the way she has come, across the spine of the country. Four hours. She sits on the sunny side and falls asleep, her backpack straps swaying from the shelf above. She thinks of Jack when she wakes.

Already she has smoothed the sharp edges, she misses his kindness. How her heart beat when she heard the car brake in the drive each evening. Could she be falling in love? It has been such a long time. She thinks: maybe. Isn't that what love is? Absorption, and anticipation, and comprehension? Learning, and daring, and forgiving all the way? A current passing between people, reinforced with the pulse each time it returns. She imagines it: glowing lines, threading each heart to the other.

Perhaps we love as we wish to be loved. A hand stroking the hair from her brow, as she strokes Jack's forehead. A man who will look after her as she does him. Jack won't stroke her brow; not yet, perhaps never. But he will listen. He will take her seriously; he makes her laugh and when she stands before him he makes her tremble.

Love takes a while. Love needs to gather its threads until they make rope.

Then she thinks: I am exiled. It is Jack's wish that she leave, that she's on this train. But every gambit brings them closer in the end, and closer to the truth.

Taking out her phone as the train nears Naples she changes the settings. A new start-up message: *Il buon tempo verrà.*

part two

# GUIDO

*Desperately loved. Can be weary of strangers.*

**FLYER SEEKING A LOST DOG**

The city is screaming. It hits her as she stumbles off the train with her bag; in the echoing cavern of the station the tannoy is going mad with announcements and there seems to be a thousand people milling on the platform. She takes one look at the station café, hoping to get a coffee; it's a melee. She heads out into the grainy sunlight. All around the entrance dingy-looking men are sitting on sleeping bags, or standing with their hands high in their jacket pockets, coolly watching. She strides determinedly into the vast space of piazza Garibaldi and its circus of traffic.

From the peace of the farmhouse to this. Her peripheral vision is crawling. Buses loom past. Street vendors, people dragging suitcases, men standing around talking, cafés spilling tables, bags of rubbish in the gutter. The noise. She plunges through the crowd, her face set, safe in her black barbaric clothes.

The cheap pensione she's booked is in a street off the far end of the piazza. She swerves around pedestrians, glad she memorised the simple route so she needn't stop and check a map. Already she can tell that in this city uncertainty means vulnerability. There is crime here, she can feel it. And yet the people are laughing, she catches broken sentences in dialect and teasing tones.

In the dingy foyer of the Hotel Fiamma a man greets her courteously. While he checks her documents he's flicking glances at her. He returns her passport and, after a few words about Australia, he offers a smile and says she's welcome to come down for a glass of wine later to plan her visit to the city. She shakes her head. 'Oh. Thank you. But I'm tired. Thank you.'

'Another time,' he says, amused by her nervousness. 'I'm a good guy, you know.' She takes her key with the correct Italian phrase of thanks and walks upstairs.

+

It takes nerve to cross the road in Naples. She emerges from the hotel, her bag gripped under her elbow, and stares at the stream of motorbikes, cars, three-wheeled miniature trucks, bicycles and wizened men tugging carts along the road at all speeds, lanes obliterated by traffic. There is no end to it; in Rome you sauntered out when there was a break, but here…She edges into the flow, it veers around her, horns blare, she keeps moving, all the time her fingernails are digging into her palms.

Only a few blocks from the hotel the feeling of the city changes. She is, according to her tourist map, on the old Roman roads that run straight across the city, and indeed they are straight and very narrow, lined with decrepit old buildings rising high over shadows. What light there is has a grainy look; the cobblestones gleam as if wet. There is such an atmosphere of decrepitude that she wouldn't be surprised if the air was full of the city itself as it puffs off walls turning to dust. From alley-ways on either side people zoom out on motorbikes bucking like ponies; the children have roughened faces, sharp mouths under long-lashed eyes. There's human shit in a portico. Every tenth building, it seems, is a baroque church with peeling ornate porch, its doors shut and chained, or open to reveal glimpses of red lamps, golden treasures. People are shouting across the street from their upstairs windows; there are stalls selling tiny Nativity scene props. She fingers a minuscule bale of hay, a toy cow, a model ruined Roman column. The shop-owner gives her a sour look from under his dirty beanie; she puts a little dog down hurriedly, and, turning away, is nearly run down by a *motorino*. The young driver yells something back at her. Across the street a woman laughs.

A grim mask settles on her face. It is her 'do not give me shit' glare. She learned it a long time ago; it's useful still. She will not be defeated by this city—though right now she feels an unfamiliar thrill that might be *actual fear*.

She finds a piazza with a church at the back, and two cafés. The tables are clean, the chairs raffia, little parasols over them despite the winter. She sinks down with relief. The waiter doesn't look insane. '*Salve,*' he says. '*Dimmi.*'

'*Un caffè,*' she says. It takes effort to move her mouth after so much clenching. '*Un caffè e un bicchi—bicchiere d'acqua, per favore.*'

He snaps his pad shut and walks off. She loves the way Italian waiters wear waistcoats. It makes her feel grand.

'*Ecco, bella signorina.*' The waiter puts her drinks down and smiles at her. The coffee is delicious. It's already getting dark; children are scrambling around a fountain nearby, and women stand in pairs and groups chatting with their hands on their hips. Naples is exactly as she'd imagined it to be. She sips her water.

So far, so good.

✦

Her room vibrates from time to time. Underground trains, she guesses. From outside her window she can hear a woman arguing. She lies on the synthetic brocade bedspread in the glare of the overhead fluorescent light and eats chocolate.

Her phone rings. 'Hello,' she says in delight.

'Hello. How are you going?'

'It's amazing. It's another world. I wish you could see it.'

He is warm on the phone. 'I was worried about you.'

'Aren't you protective? My little worrier.'

'I am. Your worrying lover. I pictured you chopped up by the side of the road.'

'I've been out for a walk. I survived, I bought pizza, and the concierge at the hotel made a pass at me. All good.'

'Don't tell me that. I don't want concierges making passes at you. What did you say?'

'I told him I have a boyfriend who'll shiv him as soon as look at him. A huge, jealous boyfriend with a cock like a fire hydrant and an unpredictable temper.'

He snorts. 'Someone I don't know about?'

'Just one of my many fans. You can't expect me to remember them all.'

'And I'm your…what? Swain?'

'My favourite swain, indeed. In his farmhouse, home from feeding the pigs.'

'This swain would like to let you know, then, that he's very jealous, as you said. And that concierges giving you compliments is all very well, but, just so you know, if you fuck someone else, it's over between us.'

'Well.' She's taken aback. What cheek! But this new possessive side is kind of exciting. So he'd be upset if she fucked someone else? What about his wife? She keeps her voice cheerful. 'I didn't know you cared so much.'

'I do care.' His voice is tense; she can tell he's amused. 'I care. And I've spent the whole day getting grey hairs worrying about you. You feel so far away.'

'I'm not. I'm right here, talking to you, lying on my bed

36

in my delightful hotel room, safe, warm and touching myself.'

'Oh. Don't do that.' His voice drops.

She is smiling like a kid but she too starts to speak lower. 'I'm naked, and I have my legs apart and I'm running my finger just very gently up and down on...'

'Don't rub your finger on yourself. Oh no, don't just slowly put the tip of your finger inside. Don't clench around it and then rub your clitoris again, don't put your hands on your breasts...'

She cradles the phone against her shoulder. All day she's been waiting for this. Her body softens as she follows his directions.

'Don't spread your legs further apart so you're completely abandoned. Don't pinch your nipples. Don't...'

'Don't grab your cock. Don't,' she sighs, 'pull your fist up and down it, slowly and firmly...'

'Oh, I would never do that—' The sound of his breath, harsh as friction down the phone. Their words are stupid. When he comes she listens with joy. She isn't finished, but after a moment he says, collecting himself, that he's glad she's okay, that he misses her, and hangs up, leaving her to pursue pleasure unencumbered, imagining his voice urging her on.

✦

She is already better at Naples. This she counts as an achievement. She has learned to storm across the road outside the hotel; to keep an easy gait that allows for veering out of the way at any second; to keep an expression on her face which is somewhere between 'buon giorno' and 'fuck off and die'. She has discovered that the people can be disconcertingly forward; three times she has been called 'bellissima signorina' and given a wink by waiters, invited out by one. Men cast their eyes over her appraisingly as they pass. People scream conversations in public. The language here is so different, their mouths are made more lasciviously, the dialect defeats her entirely. It is like another country, after Rome, after the farmhouse; she's heard it said that Africa starts south of Rome. Her eyes are so open and alert every moment that by mid-afternoon she only wants to lie down and close them.

Are people staring at her? There don't seem to be any other tourists here. She is hungry, really hungry; coffee is a sour syrup in her belly. But when she finally sees a restaurant, alone, female, she hurries past. Cafés sell only pastries and lollies. She is desperate. A pizza-by-the-slice place, thank god. What's wrong with her? Why doesn't she think she can sit down to eat? She wants to go into a gallery, but flinches at the entrance: what if a guard were to appear, and tell her the place is closed? She lingers a moment, then wanders on.

Jack would absolutely, absolutely hate Naples.

✦

The next night on the phone he says he's sorry now that she left. He was wrong to get so anxious; he was very tired, but he liked having her there. Bugger the farmer, bugger what the people at work think of him falling asleep in meetings. She's good for him. It's cold when he gets home to the empty grate and no fire.

She's pleased by this volte-face but says only that she misses him too. She hears him laughing, makes him laugh more. 'You should come here and visit me. I could show you around. We can have a weekend in this naughty city. Oh,' she sighs, 'it would be so great to be here with you.'

A hesitation, then: 'Fuck it. I will.'

'Really? Are you serious?'

'I'm taking the risk you're having me on. But I'm going to come. I could drive over Friday night.'

'I promise to spend the next four nights in utmost purity, then, to save myself for you.'

'And I'll help you buy some new clothes.'

'You will not. I like my clothes.'

'Something nice, a cardigan, a skirt below the knees…'

'Oh, you are so funny. Such a joker.'

He tells her that she is the best of his lovers; that the thought of her makes him hard in the middle of the day. But he hangs up saying only, 'Keep in touch, won't you.' As if she were some distant friend.

'Oh, I will,' she says, amused. She puts the phone down, her face wreathed with happiness; she looks at herself in the mirror, and says aloud, 'Kate, you are such a fucking sucker.'

✦

The concierge is there every night when she gets home, and every night he gives her a complicit smile and suggests she have a glass of wine with him. Guido waggles his eyebrows; he shows his white teeth, square and neat. His eyes are dangerously blue against his olive skin; his throat above the neck of his jumper is smooth and brown. She enjoys their encounters; enjoys the frisson. As she walks up the stairs he calls after her, 'I'll see you later, beautiful. Don't be scared. I won't touch you!'

The third night, home early because she's so tired, she contemplates the long evening ahead with her volume of Casanova's memoirs and the bedspread, and says yes. Just one glass of wine. She gives him a warning glance.

'*Bene.* I'll meet you in the lounge in two hours.'

She rings Jack, but there is no answer; he's probably still at work. She lies on the bed, her feet ticking over like an engine. Casanova is writing about virtue: 'An intelligent girl could only be ashamed of giving herself to a man she did not love'. He goes on: 'but if she loved me, then love, assuming responsibility for everything, would justify her in everything'. She puts it aside. In the mirror she looks tired, her skin a mask of age over a young face. The last thing she wants is to get up and walk out of the room, but she's promised.

In the hotel lounge Guido pours her a glass of young white wine. 'To your visit to Napoli.'

'To Napoli. *Che bella.*'

They talk about what she's seen, a little in Italian, mostly in English. She offers idiotic comments on the spirit of the city, he listens, sitting next to her on the old couch with his legs crossed. She says the men of Naples are interesting, predatory, impassive; she has noticed how at a certain time of day all the women disappear. 'To make dinner?'

He clicks his tongue and looks at her. 'They meet their lovers, maybe?'

She laughs. 'Probably. But then what are all the men doing out on the footpath playing cards?'

'They hope their wives don't have good time with their lovers.'

'Are you married?'

'No. I had *una fidanzata* but we…' He makes a 'breaking' gesture with his hands.

'Weren't you a bit old, for an Italian guy, to be getting married?'

He shrugs, looks sheepish.

He's a nice guy after all; those eyes are friendly, mischievous. He shifts in his seat and watches her. 'You are a nice girl. You're here alone, you like adventures. But you are a little afraid. You smile a lot. I think you have a hard time. Now you are here to have fun.'

'Yes. I'm living here, I…had a hard time before I arrived.

40

The world is still new to me. I need some nice things. Naples,' she says, unnerved by his astuteness, 'seems like a crazy place to come for fun but I like it. The streets, the air of wildness, anything could happen...'

He interrupts. '*Napoli è un casino.*' A mess. 'Keep your eyes open. Always look where you're going. You are a foreigner, you have to be careful.' He's smiling. 'I'll look out for you.'

'Thank you.' She is embarrassed. Is it that obvious that she's raw and naïve, that she puts on bravado when she stares back at the sinister men in the street, when she forces herself to enter a male-only café for a coffee? She thought she was doing well. All these men so keen to protect her. She stifles a yawn. 'Sorry.'

'Tired?'

'Yes.'

He says, 'Let me rub your shoulders.'

Oh, she thinks. Oh, it's too crass. 'No, I'm all right. Thanks.'

'No worry. I don't touch you if you don't like. Just to make you feel good.'

She refuses; he keeps offering. It gets ludicrous. In the end she says okay. Stiffly she half-turns; his hands are warm on the upper part of her arms. She giggles, but her stomach is tense.

He is talking: about Naples, about his father, who was a fashion model, went to all the famous parties in the 1960s, a very handsome man, his brother Massimo looks just like him. His hand strokes down her spine, lifts the hem of her jumper, slides beneath. She says, 'Ah, don't.'

'Just here. I won't touch you more. Just here.'

She thinks that she must say something but it is only his hand, on her back. It's only skin. Perhaps he'll stop there. She knows, as she says it to herself, that this is not true, but she can't seem to say anything more. She doesn't want to make a scene.

Stroke, stroke...his palm is warm and dry, her body is rigid with tension. 'Thank you,' she says, meaning, 'stop' but she doesn't say that word, and Guido keeps stroking. Now around the soft of her waist, now onto her belly. Yes, up to her bra, and underneath.

She has become a doll, waiting for him to release her. If she weren't blank she would be nervous. She thinks, in a minute he'll get bored, then I'll say goodnight. Her eyes are closed. She observes herself, stiff and half-toppled onto his lap, his sensuous caresses, her absurd passivity. He must know she isn't enjoying this; but then, why doesn't she say so? What's wrong with her?

The stupid foreign girl, seduced. Is she supposed to be flattered—an Italian adventure? She wishes it were Casanova, how good he'd have been at this. But is it so bad, this attention? Jack, telling her that he'd finish with her if she fucked anyone else. Jack, who won't fuck her—who can't seem to give her a compliment without a lecture as well—and this guy hasn't lectured her, has only noticed her vulnerability and seems to understand it. His hand is so hot.

So when Guido kisses her, she keeps her lips shut against his for a moment, then opens them. But her eyes are still closed.

✦

The next day she wakes to a city dank with clouds. It is stony cold; in her black shawls and coat she stalks up an incline through light that makes everything harsh, and gets the funicular train to San Martino high above the rest of the city. There is a monastery there. She is the only visitor in the vast white cloister. As the sky above clears to freezing blue she leans against a wall beside a stone skull. In the shelter of this wide space there is no wind.

Her belly is tight, her mouth sour from cigarettes. The evening scene with Guido seems unreal, a tableau: her weird blankness, her mute acquiescence, his hidden face and groping hand. Even if they only made out, didn't go all the way. *Stupid fucking girl, fucking slut.* So weak as to let a man do that as if she were so cheap, as if she were still cheap.

*Fucking moronic bitch. Thing.* She walks around the cloister with her face tight, her front teeth set.

Is it such a fallibility, being a romantic? It seems to make her a mark. It's there for all to see, even some idiot in a hotel, she might as well hang a sign around her neck: *Take advantage of me please.* The 'please' is because not only is she stupid but she's obscenely polite, too. So polite she couldn't ask someone to remove his hand from her tit.

Jack, Guido, they think she's so fey, so naïve. Her black clothes, her love of poetry, the wistfulness. Like a child. How much they love themselves, while all the time they despise her. What they don't know is that this is her survival. It's not that she's unaware of the world's perils; she knows them too well. She is clinging to the rope of romanticism like a woman hauling herself up a cliff.

The shit she's seen. She knows more about the world than either of them. But *she* is too tactful to say so; she is too intent on her lifeline. And she is stone, stone as these white marble skulls, trying to melt back into flesh.

But look at her: no independent sprite, but a pathetic woman-child throwing herself at every man who wants her. Has she rescued herself in all the wrong ways? Her muteness, her paralysis. Perhaps she's not so strong, so recovered. Perhaps all that she believes about herself is a terrible error.

Unwelcome, a memory from years before, as things started fraying and the drugs tipped her sideways, when she was frightening herself, trying to be bold. Saying to a friend, 'But don't you *want* to fuck me?' His look of shock—and pity.

She has no bloody idea what she's doing here; it seems she needs more from other people than she wanted to believe. She flinches at the thought; then hears, deep inside, a small mocking voice that says: you're running away. 'I could lie down like a tired child,' she whispers. Shelley wrote those words here in Naples. 'And weep away the life of care / Which I have borne and yet must bear…'

She leaves the high plateau of San Martino; tight as a blister with frustration, she stomps down a thousand steps to the city below, and loses herself in the streets until she is exhausted.

✛

That night Guido takes her out to dinner. She has no will to say no; she can't tell the difference anymore between blaming him and blaming herself. Wretchedness makes her pliant. After all, he is attractive. He looks at her and promises to make her feel better. He chatters away as they walk through the mad Naples evening; the noise and the chaos wake her up. Guido ushers her into a taverna and orders seafood. He gazes at her, distracts her with jokes, tells her about his childhood, makes her comfortable. Slowly her spirit animates. Here she is, in a real Naples restaurant, not some tourist place, with a Napoletano who is pleased to have her company, who pours her wine and water, who is handsome. He didn't just kiss her and dump her; perhaps he really likes her. Or most likely he wants to get his end in this time. If that's the case then she appreciates the trouble he's taking. Ah, stupid girl, be on your guard, she thinks, but he makes her laugh, and she finds she is not so sad now.

She is buoyed by this sense of being a real person in Naples, and Guido is so worldly, talking of his youth here and the crime and the drugs and the girls, all the foreign girls who come here, and the city, full of mysteries and grit. But enough of acting the innocent who needs everything explained to her. She takes a gulp of wine and says, 'I was a hooker once, you know. A prostitute?'

He raises his eyebrows.

'Yeah, I was on the streets. That's why I'm not scared here. I know it's stupid but I feel like I know these places. You know, around the station, near the hotel—it's pretty sketchy. But I've been there before. I had to be really hard, you know. I was a tough cookie.'

'*Scusa?*'

'Tough. *Brutta.*' She bares her teeth. 'Mean. Watch out.'

He laughs. 'I think so.'

'I did drugs too.' A confession, fast as a rush. 'So I'm not quite as innocent as you might think.'

'Ah, *droghe.*'

'*Eroina. Cinque anni.*' She strokes the crooks of her elbows. 'So. I like Naples. It's familiar.' She grows a little quiet, then. 'It's all over now. I wasn't a *puttana*, Guido, not really. I wasn't, how do you say, *promiscuosa?* Just work. It was just work.'

'*Ho capito. Lavoro*, work.' A dazzling smile. '*Va bene. Va bene.* I know.' He raises his glass, she clinks hers against it. 'To Napoli. *Bella Napoli.* And to you, Katie, *ragazza misteriosa.*'

'Chin chin.'

'Cheen cheen.'

He drives them back to the hotel and they go to the small concierge's bedroom. Does she want to be here? She thinks so; that is, she can't think of a reason why not. Jack? He is not reason enough. Guido is nice to look at, he has a directness and candour she appreciates. He tells her she is beautiful and he seems to understand who she is. He paid for the meal.

'You think I am a naughty guy,' he says. 'You think I just want to kiss you and touch you and then, hey, nothing. I want to kiss you and touch you, yes. Why not? You will like it too. If you don't like, you tell me. Here,' he says, and pulls off her coat, removes her shoes, her clothes piece by piece.

'I told you I have a boyfriend,' she says. *Boyfriend*? For Jack? He'd kill her to hear it. She's already naked. But it has to be said.

'And where is he, your boyfriend?'

'On the other side of the country,' she admits. 'We don't have sex much, anyway.'

'Well.' Guido stands and strips off his jumper and shirt. 'I am here. Here I am!' He pumps out his chest; strikes a pose.

He eases her onto her back. It's cold in the room. Oh, all this newness to be got through, another body to learn. She peeps at it: nice. She lies there and doesn't move; only the back of a hand tentatively strokes Guido's wrist.

He runs his hand down her chest, pausing to caress each breast. He kisses her belly. He kisses each knee. He raises his face, smiling like a kid, and blows a kiss at her. Gradually he calms her with his slow hands. Her skin grows warm. This time it is she who lifts her head to kiss him and pull him down. She thinks, Tenderness is a gift.

✦

The next morning she comes down from her own room and Guido is at the desk. He beams up at her as she descends the stairs.

'I didn't know you had to work this morning.' She is already mothering. 'You must be so tired.'

'I work, yes. But I play too.' He comes out from behind the desk, takes her hands. 'Tonight I play again.'

But Jack will call. She had already decided to tell him that her phone ran out of charge; there were four missed calls on it

46

this morning. 'Ah, I'm sorry, I can't tonight.'

'Your boyfriend?' Why does he look so amused?

'Yes. That's right. And,' she says, deliberately but smiling, 'I miss him.'

Guido shrugs. 'Of course. But—' His eyes widen. 'One moment. Here, quick.' He grabs her arm and leads her to a small door off the foyer, opens it. 'Get in.'

Confused, she enters: it's a tiny room, filled with brooms and cleaning products and someone's luggage. Guido turns away; darts back to kiss her and whispers, 'You wait here.'

From behind the closed door she hears a woman's voice, and Guido's, speaking dialect. A tone of familiarity, few greetings or farewells, then the woman leaves.

Guido comes back in and flicks on the light.

'Who was it?'

'My girlfriend.'

'Your girlfriend…you mean, now?'

He chuckles. 'Yes. I told you we broke up. In fact we are still together.'

She gazes at him, unsure how to respond. He seems amused. He expects her to understand this situation, this game; he is treating her as a player, not a dupe.

She decides to go for sophistication; shakes her head ruefully. 'You Napoletani. So many women.'

Arms around her waist. 'So many beautiful women. And this beautiful one, who I want. Who I want very much.'

His face is so handsome, his eyes glitter with arousal. It is wicked, this game; now she too is entertained by the way he'd bustled her into a cupboard, like something in a farce. The foreign girl, the secret lover, the dangerous risk. She lifts her face and kisses him.

He spins her around, presses her against the vinyl wallpaper of the little room and undoes her pants. The sex is quick and intent: his breathing in her ear, the flush of excitement to her face, and her hand, flexing against plastic wood grain in front of her, are all she remembers.

+

Jack can't come to Naples tomorrow. Too much work. 'I'm so sorry,' he adds. 'I really was going to come, you know.'

It was one thing, striding around Naples on her own, feeling independent, having this ridiculous thing with Guido; now she feels ill. She's been itemising the city for things to show him, how she's managed to domesticate this feral place. The charming corners and the grot. She had lain in bed, even this morning after the night with Guido, and thought of Jack. In her mind his restraint had become erotic. She thought of his lips near hers, not quite touching, and of the way he looked at her sometimes, knowing and enthralled. Now there won't be an adventure in Naples. And he'll be going to England to see his wife in a week.

She feels, for a moment, close to panic.

'I won't say I wish you didn't have to work. I know you do. But I wish you could come.'

'I know.' A sigh. 'But the meeting yesterday—these bloody idiots, Nick hadn't done the assessment and really it's part of my responsibilities, I can't even let it sit until Monday. What's going to be really murderous is the listings...'

Responsibility. Assessment. Listings. 'Oh Jack,' she says.

He takes it for sympathy. 'I know, it's a mess. Listen, you'll be all right, won't you? On your own?'

'Sure. I love Naples. I'm having fun.'

'Are you warm enough? I thought perhaps you should buy a warm coat. Something nice, maybe with fur.'

'Jesus, I can't buy fur.'

'Of course you can. You have to stop thinking like a student—'

'Fur! Apart from anything else, I have hardly any money—'

'—dress your age. You have to give away this fantasy that you're not a grown woman. Look at you. You're in Naples, surviving—from what you tell me, which isn't much—on your own, you're bright, nice-looking—' she rolls her eyes, '—and you're what, thirty years old?'

'Twenty-*nine*.'

She is abruptly bored. Perhaps he's right, why shouldn't she have a nice warm coat? Naples is made of ice, her shoulders are permanently hunched against the chill. She's watched the Italian women, their sleek leather boots, their thick hair and buckled handbags.

'It's about respect for yourself,' he's saying. 'If you don't have that, you can't expect other people to respect you.'

'I know that.'

'For example,' he goes on, 'my wife respects herself. My god, almost to a fault. She's given me hell sometimes. And I have the greatest respect for her. She's a magnificent woman.'

How can he do it, how can he say this to her? He is monstrous—or she is weak to be hurt by it. 'So you keep telling me.' Resentment heats her face. 'Do you know, a few days ago you said you loved me. Now you respect your wife so much. So much—' she can feel a choking in her throat, '—so much that you won't come and see me, even though you said you would.'

'I told you. I have to work.'

'But I knew you wouldn't come. You—'

'It's childish, this attitude. I said to you before you left that I hope I can trust you. I hope I made the right decision. I wonder if I have.'

It's so unfair. The first time she's really challenged him and he threatens the whole thing.

'I've always been honest with you. I've told you everything about how I feel. Talk about respect and trust…I've taken that risk, I respect you but *you*, Jack, you can't, that's why—'

'*This* is exactly *why* I have reservations about you.' She pushes down her outrage, makes herself listen. 'I don't want fights. I want peace. I just want to have a nice time with you, whom I like very much when you're not behaving like a child, and I want you to be safe and to become the woman you could be, if you'd just stop *arguing* and analysing everything. You think about *everything*, Kate, you want to pick me to pieces, and it gets tiring.'

She is silent.

Then he says, 'Don't be upset. I know you wanted me to come and see you. Believe me, I'm flattered. And I really was looking forward to it. I worry about you.'

'I know you do.' She lies back on the bedspread, exhales. He wants her to be brave. And yet if she fakes a smile, covers the tremor, clenches her fists in secret, she is insincere. She is a liar.

'I'll ring you tomorrow. And I'll be slaving away alone in the office all weekend, so if you wanted to, you could ring me then and talk to me and, you know, you could help this interfering old man feel good. You're very sexy on the phone, Kate.'

Despite herself, she says. 'Am I?'

'Very good. In fact, right now, you're making something happen…'

She slips a hand into her pants with a combination of boredom and gratification. 'Oh yes?'

✦

The next morning she wakes and realises that the idea of another day in Naples is awful. It's too cold. She doesn't have the energy to go shopping for that coat. The streets are full of bruising glances and the threat of being run down by a vehicle. All that battling.

Jack's banished her. Guido: perhaps it's better not to get in further with him. The whole thing feels a little off-kilter, a little mad. She doesn't quite understand it. When in doubt, do nothing, her mother always told her. Do nothing.

Fuck it, she'll go back to Rome. It's not a defeat. It's a stratagem.

Guido isn't at the desk when she pays her bill.

She wants to be truthful, but she wants to be loved too, she must be strong to be lovable, how can she be strong when she feels alone? It is beginning to seem, she thinks miserably on the train home along the bleak littoral, that it is all bitterly incompatible.

✦

Her bed in Rome is a tiny single one, it would be snug for a child. It is in the spare room of a furnished flat rented by Tom, a friend of a friend. She'd arranged to stay here for a while, not sure how long, a month, two? It's already been one and a half. Tom is a bluff man in his sixties, trim, with arms that have done a million tight-lipped press-ups, with skin toughened by the elements, and an unexpectedly excellent sense of humour. It was he who took her to a work party, who introduced her to Jack. The two men have known each other for years.

She and Tom had lived together for a month before she went south to fuck his friend: beers in the evening, bowls of pasta and sauce, huge bottles of cheap wine, chain-smoking conversations. He pretended she was the kind of housemate he'd wanted; she pretended she wasn't an inconvenience. The system worked well.

Now she finds him sitting in the lounge room on the ugly

51

brown vinyl couch, watching *BBC World News*, an ashtray and a couple of empty stubbies beside him. 'Ay oop,' he says. 'Where you been, girlie?'

'Och aye,' she says, and disappears to dump her bag in her room. 'I told you. Down south. Out and about. Down and out. It's okay, isn't it, if I stay here again for a while?'

He gives her a look. 'You left your crap in the bedroom. You owe me rent. There's a kitchen floor that needs mopping.'

'It would be my honour,' she says, and when he asks if she wants a beer she says, 'Oh fuck, yes please, you're grand,' and they watch the news together, and she doesn't have to explain anything.

✦

She is on her way to the Caelian hill. The park there is a refuge, its tall umbrella pines stand like sentinels over empty grass, shrubs, some old Roman fragments and benches where women nurse babies. The place is always quiet and even in winter it catches the sun. The plane trees that line the street are bare and their branches pale brown, as if burnt. On her way to the park's ornamental entranceway, she sees that the little church nearby is, for once, open; she enters and is the only person inside. In a relentless fresco all around the curved wall are martyrs, being horribly killed: disembowelled, toasted, decapitated and pincered. It is a warning, she supposes, to the people; or an inspiration? She has a bit of the martyr in her, she reflects dryly. There is something she can understand in this rapturous giving away of the self, of perishing shrieking and ecstatic in flames, in the hope of a better life. It's a shame she's not at all religious; she would be so good at it.

A sign points down some stairs to the crypt. The steps are slippery; the stone walls become suddenly rough; she descends several metres and she is two thousand years in the past. A Roman building is nestled below, like one half of an eggshell resting in another.

There is someone else here. A young man raises his head as she enters a room. '*Ciao*.'

'*Ciao*.'

She wanders the empty, damp rooms, their low ceilings lit by fluorescent strips. The cold makes her head ache. She tries to summon an idea of banquets, of people in tunics and togas walking through this very door, leaning against this wall now stripped to mortar, grey with age. The young man reappears and watches her as she gazes at a lump of masonry.

'It is not very interesting.'

She turns. 'It's a bit empty. And cold. *Fa freddo*.'

'I am an archaeologist. Let me show you something.'

She follows him through the maze of tiny doors and confused spaces. 'An archaeologist? I wanted to be an archaeologist.'

'Truly? Then you will like this. I am finding it.'

He beckons her through a door so low she has to duck, and past some barrier tape. 'See.'

There are marble paving tiles still in place, and in the middle a worn crag of stone. 'This is what I found. It is a Mithraeum, a religious sanctuary. See? There are benches still, for the worshippers to sit.'

She knows about the Mithras cult, how it was the template of Christianity, down to the ritual sacrifice and the redemption; they talk about the sect and archaeology and how he has found this place but there is no money to protect it so he has been instructed to concrete it over until another year, when perhaps there will be money, and how sad he is and she agrees that Rome is full of marvels but, she says, it is hard when you're alone and the city is so big, and when he asks her out for a coffee it seems a good thing to say yes.

'My name is Federico,' he says, holding out his hand. He is genial. His little dark beard, snub nose and earnest face remind her of someone she knew in Melbourne. They drink coffee in the sunshine outside a bar and she finds herself talking freely of her loneliness, of the strangeness of being in a new city. He isn't from Rome himself but a small town in the north; they compare notes on exile. He listens kindly and even when he says that he is single and also, sometimes, lonely, there is not a hint of approach. His apartment, he says, is so full of books he can hardly move. They have read the same European classics; he loved Keats when he was younger. She quotes Byron: 'O Rome! My country! city of the soul!' careless of how silly it sounds. He is not sexy, or predatory, he gives her no compliments or offers for shoulder massage, only a smiling sense that he is *simpatico*. The afternoon goes quickly now; she won't make it to the park, but she returns home lively with the sense that she has found a friend. Perhaps this is how real life here begins.

✛

Three nights before Christmas, Tom looks at her over a glass of wine and says, 'I'm off tomorrow night. Did I tell you? Going skiing in Austria. Thought you might like to come.'

'I can't ski.'

He snorts. 'Somehow I'm not surprised. Well, you can learn. I'm taking the night train.'

She tips her own glass, drains the wine; she thinks, Try what I don't know, try what scares me. 'Why not?' she says, 'Count me in.'

But when they flop into the hotel room in Austria the morning before Christmas Eve she immediately climbs into bed, exhausted, and he heads off to the slopes. She imagines he'll be back in an hour or two; they'll go out together, and she'll find out what a ski slope looks like; how to strap on skis and move; how to see in a world so white. She has seen snow only once before when she was a child, and that was just a sprinkle; she doesn't even know how to walk on the stuff. Her boot has a hole in the sole. A fear takes her: she won't be able to breathe out there in the thin air. She lies in bed all day reading. Tom says nothing when he returns in the late afternoon except that she'd missed out on a great day. The next morning when he wakes her up she pulls the covers over her head and hides.

There is no food served in the hotel while the guests are out on the slopes; the heating is turned down. It is very quiet. She doesn't turn on the lamps but sits at the window staring out at the white world. Where would she go? How would she get there? All the people she can see passing by are dressed in fluorescent yellow and pink and blue; her clothes are all black. She longs for a hot blue-skied Australian morning so suddenly and fiercely that tears spill from her eyes.

In her mind she sees herself crouching in Guido's embrace. How much she had needed tenderness; and how ashamed she was of that need the next day, that she'd been so cheap: how great her need was. She had worried that he was mocking her with his embraces. In the bare-lit chilly room, alone in the hotel apart from the staff, belly empty, she cries.

Tom hurts his leg that day; they eat Christmas Eve dinner in a dining room loud with festive skiers. She is so humiliated she barely speaks but appreciates Tom's cheerful banter. Christmas is jolly and wintry and fir-treed here; all around her people speak French and German and Italian, and they eat heavy puddings and not a single person wishes her merry Christmas except for Tom. Neither of them gives the other a gift. They board the train home on Boxing Day so Tom can fly off on leave the next morning. She stands in the train corridor, staring for eight hours out of the window, at a world obliterated by snow in a way she had never imagined, and thinking that she is a long way from home and not as brave as she'd bloody thought.

✦

She had once fallen in love with a young man who loved her too. The two of them were inseparable; they talked all day, shared their passions, embraced, cried with each other, they made their own small glowing world in the cone of light beside his bed. The only times she felt lonely were when he fucked her, because the sex was almost always bad; and when he was fucking other women, and then she wept.

He knelt beside her one day, as she crouched on his floor, and asked why she cried.

'Because I want you to love me. And you won't, and you love all of them so much more. I can never be like them. I'm not made like that—I'm not fiery and wild and confident and sexy. And you know it. You despise me for it. I'm going to lose you.' She couldn't explain how it corroded, to offer her body, so naked, and be refused.

He reached down and raised her. 'But, you bloody idiot, I love you. I always will. Don't you see? I can fuck them, and love you more.'

And, though it hurt like hell, she learned it was possible to parse 'love'.

✦

Four days before the New Year, Guido texts her: *Ciao bella why don't you visit before you see boyfriend?* She rings him.

How lovely of him to invite her, but she says she doesn't

want to lie to Jack, not outright. If she stopped in Naples on the way she'd have to mention it and he would want to know why.

'I have to lie to my girlfriend.'

'And?'

'So what does it matter? They don't know, they don't care.'

She thinks. Jack is always telling her to be independent. Might that not mean self-sufficient? And isn't self-sufficiency freedom? What claim does Jack have anyway—today he's getting home from seeing his *wife*. She hates to feel owned; she hates possessiveness. By playing this game, surely she can practise for winning the one with Jack?

'Kate, *bella*...'

'Maybe. Maybe I'll come.'

✦

She sits on a bench in a park, surrounded by headless Roman statues, and tries to understand why she hates those who want her. There is a flinty watcher behind her living eyes, that sees them in desire—the way those men grow ugly, even as they grow gentle with beautiful feeling; the ridiculous act of sex; the humiliation of their pink pricks standing out from their bodies. She presses her lips in disgust. It's much easier to pretend it is not real; that she herself is not humiliated by her body's wet crevice, the ease with which it is penetrated, her own willing renunciation of dignity. And the games. The games are so tedious but she is grateful for them too: they keep things unreal. Just a dance, a skirmish.

Perhaps she punishes men. She offers herself as a decoy. The very thing they think they win is their undoing. Then when they are unmasked she can see clearly how little they mean to her. Let them grope her, lecture her, patronise and teach her, let them gasp gratitude for her skin, her kindness. None of them,

57

none, knows how cold she is, how she doesn't forgive.

Byron, oh, he knew what it was to hate.

> There was in him a vital scorn of all:
> As if the worst had fall'n which could befall,
> He stood a stranger in this breathing world,
> An erring spirit from another hurl'd;
> A thing of dark imaginings, that shap'd
> By choice the perils he by chance escap'd;
> But 'scap'd in vain, for in their memory yet
> His mind would half exult and half regret...

And so Jack accuses her of being romantic? Not so. She is using him. Relentlessly, she acknowledges this. Sex is currency; it is validation; it's the most debased form of tender and exchangeable at favourable rates. Guido seems to understand this and not mind. But he's just a happy fool.

Is she a free spirit or a loose cannon? Is she pursuing freedom? Or caught in the same old trap?

'Face it,' she says to herself on the bench. 'What you are is a neurotic pain in the arse.'

✦

The phone rings. '*Ciao*, it is Federico, the archaeologist.'

'*Ciao*, Fred!' She is delighted to hear from him. He is so sweet and serious and shy. Already she feels they are friends. They spring into conversation, they talk of books and history and his Mithraeum, they talk of friendship and the importance of having the right people in your life. He tells her what he's cooking for dinner and she asks him if it's true that palazzo Venezia is made from bits of the Colosseum. He knows her favourite statue in the city, Madama Lucrezia, neglected in a corner with ancient wise eyes and a mouth blunted off by the elements. She knows of the hidden Mithraeum at the end of Circus Maximus. It's too easy, talking for an hour. When he says he is about to leave to see his family for New Year's Eve she is sorry to hear it.

It has occurred to her that if she had a female friend things might be better. There is little prospect of one. The young women of Rome are clenched with haughtiness—or apprehension. Their lithe bodies, with wrists narrow as children's, seem adamantine, so thin and hard; their beautiful mouths stretch and grimace as they speak; they cast cool hostile gazes at her if they deign to see her at all. They will walk right into her, deliberately oblivious: every encounter is a test, and she doesn't know how to meet it. The older women are worse: thickened now, their pretty faces grown squat, they stare at her with implacable hatred, and do not break their intent watching even when she gives them a matching contemptuous flick of the eyes; she can feel their envy of her youth like a scorch.

The women won't talk to her. The men are all too happy to talk, and more. The women sense that she is a slut. They are afraid she'll steal their boyfriends—Hah, she thinks, you bitches, I do.

✦

On the living room table, a pile of books: her salvation. *The Story of My Life* by Casanova, *Selected Poems* of Byron, *An Oxford Archaeological Guide to Rome*, Goethe's *Italian Journey*, Tacitus' *History*, *Teach Yourself Latin*, *The Literary Guide to Rome*, Eleanor Clark's *Rome and a Villa*.

A biography of Shelley, a leather notebook into which she's been transcribing Romantic poetry. She notes street names, checks a map, lists addresses. She's not the first to lose herself in Rome; not the first to be overwhelmed. As Shelley said, 'The life can burn in blood, even while the heart may break.'

Shelley's house in via del Corso shouldn't be too difficult to find. There it is, when she lumbers up the street, battling crowds on the narrow pavements. It is a large pale building, not unlike the others to each side, traffic passing in front of it. The Shelleys lived here in 1819; a plaque says so. The door is closed; no sign whether the apartment remains, no invitation to enter. She imagines Mary Shelley here, returning exhausted after a tedious salon at one of the ex-pat dens, her husband beside her, talking too loudly as usual, making the passing Italians stare. She imagines Claire Clairmont, walking behind, casting wistful looks in case her lover Byron should appear, or jealously watching Shelley. She imagines all the tension in that house, how each would have been wrapped in thought as they passed through that door, how badly it would all soon end. Shelley seeing his double, just before his death, and the double asking, 'How long do you mean to be content?'

It's a question she would like to ask herself; but she's not content yet.

Goethe's house is there too, further up the street. It is a museum. She pays and enters. An eighteenth-century house, the ceiling of the third floor carefully restored, its timber beams, its painted decoration. Wide windows with shutters and a display on the life of the poet. A brochure tells her that this is certainly the address where Goethe stayed with his friend Tischbein but not, perhaps, the right rooms. 'This city is such a great school,' the gleeful writer had exclaimed. 'Though I am still always myself, I believe I have been changed to the very marrow of my bones.'

From one of the glass cases, she copies out a letter from an unknown woman to the young Goethe during his escape to Rome.

I'd like to know why you went away like that last
night without a word I am your sweetheart if only you
could love me like I love you I hope to have a good
reply it is not like I thought goodbye goodbye.

Goethe confided to his diary, 'The more I see of this city,
the more I feel myself getting into deep waters.'

There is the Keats–Shelley museum in the piazza nearby, of
course. It is closed for renovations. Opposite it, according to her
notes, is the palazzo where Byron stayed, at number 66. Appro-
priate for the old half-devil. She stands tentatively in the arched
doorway that leads to the entrance corridor. Byron stood here
too, he really passed through this space. For a moment she holds
this in her mind; but then the tourists barge too near, the dream
is lost. Across the piazza is a shirt shop called 'Byron'; here, in
the palazzo, there is no plaque.

Anyway, all these buildings are closed to her.

She sits on the Spanish Steps a few metres away. Around her,
tourists chatting, laughing, flirting. In her black leather coat she
watches them and balefully smokes.

She hauls herself up the steps to the top of the hill and
turns right into a dark, narrow street. Past a massive hotel, flags
and brass doorway; the porters look at her superciliously as she
blunders past. There—is it the right number, it's hard to see in
the gloom—yes, that's it—the other place the Shelleys stayed.
The Romantic poets adored Rome but they spent little time
here. It was all in their imagination. No plaque. No sign. The
massive door of the grim old palazzo is, of course, resolutely
closed. She takes a photograph of it, just because.

She'll leave no trace here, either. She can live as fiercely
as she will, it's only breath smoking glass. A million people
have trod these streets already and scarcely worn the stones.

She exists, perhaps, only as the blurred, sullen figure in the background of a thousand tourist snapshots, her face closed, already moving out of frame.

✦

Time leaks through, drop by drop. Two days until the new year. In the apartment she finds herself wandering the rooms, a cup of cold coffee in her hand. She should go out; the idea terrifies her. Down the stairs? Into that grim light? And then where? She pictures herself, hurrying through streets she has already walked a hundred times, always as if urgently striding somewhere. A stroll through the *centro* becomes a race to its exterior. The nest of the centre won't hide her. The apartment will. Defeated, she walks into the kitchen; into the lounge room; there is nothing waiting for her there. She should ring someone, but who? Jack is away. Tom is away. Federico is away. Guido will be with his girlfriend. It's too late in the day now to ring Melbourne; she has no phonecard; it costs too much. The nearest internet café is a train ride away. She doesn't know what she'd say, anyway.

Is she getting it right? Is she getting it wrong? How do you recover? How do you recognise trauma? Or is she just pissing about, tripping over her own ego, fucking things up?

She needs someone to tell her she's okay. But she can't bear to be with anyone; she escaped them all, crossed the world to do it.

The memory of their pity, their concern, of doubt in herself. She packed it and brought it with her, after all.

Fear gapes. She stands at the sink, her hands loose in soapy water, and shudders with tears.

It feels as if she is becoming damp, sodden, like newspaper soaking up a spill until it shreds. Outside the rain starts again.

She smokes one more cigarette. On the stereo Ella Fitzgerald mourns, 'A man is born to go a lovin', a woman's born to weep and fret'. *Black Coffee*. There is no milk in the fridge; black coffee it is.

She is drinking her third cup of the day, promising herself again that she'll go out, though it's already two o'clock and it'll get dark at four, when the phone rings. She runs to answer it.

Jack is back from England, but she can't come to see him for New Year's Eve tomorrow. He's concerned that the farmer will notice her and gossip in the village. He knows it's stupid but he has to think of his job, his peace. 'You'll be okay, won't you?'

She has been holding on for the moment he will ring her, for the moment she will get off the train and he will walk towards her. It was the one definite point in the weeks ahead. She breathes shallowly, like someone controlling deep pain.

'I can't come?'

'Well, like I said, it's difficult. It's only a night, anyway. Such a long way to come. You can stay in Rome, you'll be fine.'

'I *won't*.' Invisible to him, her face is crumpling. Oh god, she's like a child. But she is frightened by her fear.

'Kate?'

'Can't I come and see you?'

'Are you okay?'

'I'm sorry.' She's crying now. It's because she'll cry at such a gentle question that makes her cry more. 'I just really want to see you.'

'I know. Me too. Just not tomorrow.'

'I don't mean to sound so upset.' But she lets herself gasp into the phone. She wants him to know. 'I'm miserable. Sorry. I'm strong, really I am. It's just…I need someone to talk to, be nice to me. Rome is h-hard. I'm all on my own, I'm just, you know…' She is crying so noisily that she can't hear

63

if he's murmuring comfort. She suddenly imagines him, horror-stricken at this performance. She weeps harder. 'You must think I'm so weak.'

'No.' He doesn't sound horrified. 'I know things are hard for you. You are strong, you're going to be fine.'

More tears spill, hot as martyrs' flames. 'I don't understand. If you love me, if you care for me, what do you care what the fucking farmer thinks? You're always so conscious of what "society" thinks. Fuck them!' Love *me*, she thinks. *Please*, love *me*.

'You don't understand. I have to think of it.'

Anger. Ah, that's better. 'You can't have me there but you say Rome is too far to come.'

'It's a long way, Kate. It's a seven-hour drive.'

Injury, too, spreads warmth through her. 'I'll come to you! Jesus, Jack, I'm trying to make this easy for you.'

'No. And don't shout at me.'

'You won't be seen with me in public but staying in together makes you claustrophobic. We can't meet in person but you reckon phone calls are too expensive; you say you care for me but you don't want any responsibility; you don't like it when I'm childish and meek but when I crack it you say don't shout at me. What the fuck is the chance that any of this is going to work?'

'Maybe none.'

They are silent.

'Listen. You're upset. I'm only just back from the airport. Go and make a cup of tea—' how stunningly English, '—and then go out. It's no good you skulking, I'm always telling you. Go out, see something lovely. Read one of your bloody poems, but not a miserable one. I do care for you, you know, I care very much. I enjoy your company immensely. I don't want you to be unhappy. You're lovely when you're happy.'

64

He's tired. She's tired. She is sorry that she raised her voice. He wants to help her but he can't. It is a lot to put on someone, just home from visiting his wife, just off a plane, a man like Jack who hates confusion and mess. She's swamping his boat. If only she could be happy and attractive and lovely, not this wretched waif with a face messy from crying and a voice piteous as she says, 'I'm sorry.'

'Don't be sorry. Just buck up. You don't want to end the year like this. Look after yourself. We can talk tomorrow night. I have to go and make dinner now. Old man, on his own…'

She could say, 'Then *don't* be, don't be on your own, what do you *want*?' but wiping her nose she says only, 'You're almost as much of an orphan as I am.'

✦

Later that night, after more crying and drinking wine and singing along to Ella, she rings him back. She is operatic with grief.

'Please, please, can't I come?'

'Oh, god. What will happen if you don't?'

'I don't know. I just feel…I feel like I'm going mad. I don't… Like I'm slipping off a cliff, and no one will even notice. Please, Jack.' She has never been so desperate, so willing to forfeit her dignity. 'Can't I come just for the night?'

He laughs. 'You're incredible. Surely it can't be as bad as all that?'

'It is. I've never been so fucked up.' *Fucked up*, what a way to put it; maybe it's the lack of fucking that has her in this state. She manages to laugh too through her tears. 'Honestly. I've been fucked up in my time but this takes the cake.'

'Well.' He sighs. 'This is the last time you manipulate me.'

She quietens. 'I don't mean to. I'm trying not to.'

'Just get the train tomorrow. I'll pick you up, and bring you back to Rome the next day. We'll have a wonderful, miserable night together.'

'Don't say that. It'll be so good to see you. But thank you.' She is wretched in her humiliation. 'Thank you, Jack.'

'Oh well. Happy New Year.'

✦

On the train, all the way back to the south. When she'd woken that morning, sober, she contemplated not going. The mortification—how embarrassing it will be to face Jack like this—but imagining the long day alone and the lonely night ahead, she resolved to go. She'd never hear the end of it if she changed her mind. It's a busy train, she is lucky to get a seat on New Year's Eve. The weather is heavy: dark clouds over the mountains and the sea, grim as granite. The train shoots her south, across the width of the country through the mountain tunnels, and then south further to the station. A seeping of sadness makes her face look long in the train window. She wonders if Jack will think she was having him on. He won't see how she really feels, this mad engulfing terror. She already knows that she will have to pay for this reprieve.

He finds her outside the station in the car park, as arranged; a discreet rendezvous. A peck on the cheek, English-style; they get into the car. They drive through the black landscape, the olives looming white in the headlights. It is very cold. She warms her hands under her thighs. She has hardly touched him. Her skin feels as brittle as shellac. He jokes about how much money he's spent on the phone to her, how she's invited herself down to gatecrash his party of one.

She wants to say, Please don't, don't laugh at me, I'm not up to it. But she goes along with the jokes, eager to make this good, and watches him, his handsome face. At least he is smiling.

They pull up outside the house and he cuts the engine. He looks at her, then, with a wide, genuine smile—that grin— 'Hello, Kate. Hello.'

He leans across and kisses her; she responds fiercely. She is full of fire, his hands clutch her and pull her onto him. Ah, he wants her, he really wants her.

Inside, he's laid a fire and gets it going in a minute. There is a bottle of wine open and two glasses; she pours, hands him one, they stand. 'Chin chin,' he says, and weak with relief and lust she smiles, kisses him again, and raises her glass. 'To the end of the year. And new beginnings.'

They talk, laugh, drink, eat olives and salami and cheese just as they used to. The same fire, the same wine. She is recovered. It was so easy. 'See,' she dares, 'it was good that I came down.'

'It is.' He is a little drunk. 'It's very good to see you. It's the best. It's the most wonderful thing in the world.'

Is he mocking her? 'I know it's weird, with us,' she says. 'But sometimes it is so wonderful.'

'You're lovely like this.' He reaches out, cups her head and brings her mouth to his. 'Sometimes—not now—your face is hard. I think you caught it just in time.'

When they make love he is strong, intent. The wine has had its effect: he's ardent but not entirely erect. She doesn't mind. Her body, for once, seems wholly present; she can locate pleasure inside, breathe upon it with her concentration, make it glow like an ember until it flares through her, and she comes violently, tears in her eyes as she loosens and curls next to him; he holds her and she feels, finally, at rest.

Midnight passes unnoticed.

As they go to bed she says, 'I know you won't be like this

in the morning. It's okay. So I will thank you now. For this.'

But in the morning he is still kind. 'Stay there,' he tells her as he rises. When he calls her to come, rumpled in his too-big dressing-gown, she finds that he has laid breakfast for them. A pot of coffee and another of warm milk, bread and jam and salami, a bowl of hardboiled eggs. 'So English,' she laughs. 'But I see, my dear, you've gone a bit native.' She picks up some salami and bites it.

'Well,' he says, sitting, 'one has to make an effort.'

'Doesn't one just.'

They set off after breakfast. For discretion's sake she hunches below the dashboard as they drive through the olive fields, but she doesn't mind, the absurdity makes her laugh. 'Can't be too careful, I suppose,' she says, straightening up once they turn onto the main road. She twists to look back at their path through the olive grove, the one that had appeared so spectral and radiant the night of the full moon.

'Yes. You have to be careful.'

It's as good a place to start as any. 'I don't want you to think I'm bunging this on,' she says. 'I wasn't manipulating you. I know you're careful of your security and I would never want to jeopardise that. I have to be careful too. Like, how much I care for you; how much I show you of myself. I've got to protect myself, as you say. But then, I don't want to be "careful" with what I tell you. That's no good. I want to be myself, to show you what I'm really like. Otherwise what's the point?'

'I want you to be yourself. That's what I'm always—'

'So can I tell you what's been going on?' She tries to find the words. 'I don't think you're the same as me, you don't get this kind of huge, swallowing fear. It's fear, Jack. I'm not just sad. I feel so small and so much like a ghost—Rome is the kind of city where you don't exist. I can walk among people all day and no one will say a word to me. If I sit on a bench, some bloke will come and bother me, but that's not what I want. And the women won't even look at me. So it's easy to start feeling weird, to begin to feel like you're not real.' There are tears running down her face, she feels wet all through. 'And then I start being sad, and the sadness gets worse, and then I realise no one knows or cares, anything could happen to me and they won't know—my family is far away, I can't call them— and so it's just me, working myself up into a state—I can't explain how terrifying it is—and you're the only person I have, you see.'

The road ahead is straight. She talks on, hearing herself complaining, trying to express just how rotten with panic she is. How the earth itself seems to be rocking her, shrugging her off.

'It's self-indulgent,' he says after some time. 'This unhappiness. You said it yourself, you work yourself up into a state. You can decide not to do that.'

'I *said* you're not like me. You don't have the same tendencies, you're not an introvert.'

'Ah, I'm not a precious romantic poetry reader.'

'I don't mean that. We're very different. But surely you can understand that I'm sincere, at least? I'm not trying to be miserable. I just am.'

'I don't flog dead horses.'

She stares at the road, her cheeks wet. 'What do you mean?'

'I mean, I have a great deal of faith in you, Kate, but I don't want to put energy into someone who doesn't want to fix themselves. I don't need the trouble.'

A million outraged words cram her throat. 'Do you realise,' she says through her teeth, 'how brave I am? How fucking brave I'm trying to be?'

'Are you?'

This is excruciating. How can he be so cruel? 'Yes, I fucking am. You don't know how tough I've had to be. You know nothing, nothing about who I am. And you're *mean*.'

'Calm down.' He speaks as if he is the most reasonable man in the world. The car speeds along the autostrada; they are in a bubble. If only she could leap free of it. She shuts up, presses her hands into the seat on either side of her. 'You over-analyse everything, you think all the time; *stop thinking!*'

She bites her lip and looks away.

'Make a plan of action. Decide what you want. I'm not going to abandon you, if that's what you think I'm doing, but you have to make this work on your own, I can only help so much.'

A stiff upper lip, that's what he's recommending. Pull your-self together. Isn't this what she wanted?

'I'm here. Anytime you need me. If you really need me and you're not just turning it on.'

'I don't turn it on,' she says.

'Don't be all sulky, it doesn't suit you. I despair of you, but I'll only give up if I think you're being self-indulgent and not really trying.'

She takes a long shaky breath. 'I will try. I don't want to be like this. It's humiliating.'

'Then don't be.' He stares at the distance ahead. The road to Rome is a long one.

✦

On the second day of the year, standing in the valley of the ancient Forum, staring at the columns in the damp and cold, a woman asks if she'll take a photo of her against the view.

'You're Australian?'

'Oh, so are you.' The woman poses. 'I thought I was the only chick here on her own.'

Click. 'Here you go, I hope it comes out okay. No, you're not the only one.'

They fall to talking. Penny is in Rome for only a week and leaving tomorrow. The cold seeps up through the marble paving and into their bones. 'Imagine,' the other woman says as they walk out, 'how cold the Romans must have been here in their togas, the poor freezing things. Their bare knees!' Penny is fifty, but has the spritely energy of a teenager. She suggests they get a coffee.

How wonderful to find another female; it's been two months now since she talked to a woman. Another outsider. Penny lives in Sweden with her academic lover, twenty years older than she, after a life of adventures, surprises, illness, glamour and addresses in several countries.

'Weren't you scared?'

Penny giggles. 'I probably should have been. I mean, if I'd had any sense. You know how it is, you just make a decision, and then the next thing comes along and you decide that, and before you know it you're miles from where you started...'

'I'm envious.'

'Don't patronise yourself. You have a real sensitivity. You think about *why* things are the way they are; not everyone does that. Feeling and caring are the most important things in the world. I'm sure you know what you're doing.'

'I can't tell you,' she says, 'how nice it is to meet someone who doesn't want to lecture me. You think I'm on the right track?'

'People always like to squash bright sparks. They can't help it. Don't let them. After all,' Penny sips her coffee, 'they might learn something from *you*.'

She asks her what it's like to move to Europe permanently—and for love. It sounds so romantic. Penny describes her lover who sounds lugubrious and controlling in a silent, deadly way.

'Reminds me of my friend Jack,' she says. 'Does he give you a look like—?' She mimes eye-rolling disappointment, prim lips.

'Yes…'

'And then this?' Jack's sorrowful concern.

'Exactly.'

'And then says that it's for your own good that he's just spent an hour telling you why you're entirely wrong about everything?'

'Yes!'

'They might be cousins.'

'Worse, they might be typical.' The two women snort.

'He treats me well most of the time, when he's not sulking,' Penny goes on. 'But it's as if he forgets that I'm a person—a person who's given up her life back home to be with him. It's all always his way, the way he likes it, when he wants it.' What a disappointment; she had inevitably imagined a kind of Max von Sydow figure against a wall of books, cosy lamplight, offering a glass of wine. 'He likes,' Penny's voice drops, '—he likes to fuck me when I have a fever.'

'What?'

'When I'm sick. He says I'm warmer.' She blushes. 'Inside.'

She sits back. 'How,' she doesn't want to say *monstrous*, 'strange.'

Penny shrugs. 'Well. He'd say I do all sorts of unfair things to him. I'm sure I do.'

'Maybe we're all bad for each other,' she says gloomily.

'No. No, we're not.' Penny clutches her arm. 'It's been so good for me talking to you. Please, whenever you want, come

72

and visit me in Sweden. Come in summer. You can stay in our cabin and wash every day in the lake. Please, tell me you will.'

The other woman seems so fervent. How lonely is Penny? As lonely as she is? But for years, years living far from home. She shakes off thinking what that might be like. 'I will. I'd love to. Oh, I wish you weren't leaving tomorrow. I finally find a girlfriend, and you have to go.'

'Have faith in yourself,' Penny says as they say goodbye. 'It's not a crime to have imagination, or think too much, or use your intuition. Don't let them tell you it is.'

They grip in a pledge of fortitude against the misunderstanding universe. 'Feeling and caring.'

'Feeling and caring.'

She walks home smiling, as satisfied as if she'd met a new lover—perhaps better, because Penny wanted nothing from her, diminished nothing, only reflected.

+

After the solitude, more solace. Federico returns. They meet in Campo de' Fiori at a merry café amid market stalls. For a twenty-eight-year-old he has a touch of old-man solemnity; she smiles to see him wearing a cardigan under his corduroy jacket. He was, she is sure, a library geek at school just as she was. For some reason she'd expected all Italian men to be suave or doltishly fashionable; this is a nice surprise. She feels a sisterly protection of him, even as they walk around a city he knows far better than she does. With him she's back at the Forum on a parapet looking down: a sight in which she can still scarcely believe.

'Where was Cicero's house on the Palatine?'

'Over there, on the far corner, until Clodius had him thrown out of Rome.'

'Where was the Lacus Curtius?'

'Behind the Rostra, in the middle there. It's where a soldier called Marcus Curtius pledged to save the city by leaping in to a mysterious lake and vanishing.'

'*Dio mio*, you are good.'

Down among the ruins they both pause at the altar of Julius Caesar and admire the flowers left there to wither. Moved, they pace on in silence.

They walk and talk all afternoon, about politics, solitude, love of learning. She finds herself making Roman-style shrugs, grimaces, exclamations, knowing that they are ridiculous. She puts more and more of her rudimentary Italian into use; Federico, to her amazement, seems to understand her mumbles. They are so busy talking that they find they have walked all the way back to her flat.

'Do you want to come in?' She hopes he hears this for what it is, a friendly invitation only. He accepts. It's very cold and she opens a bottle of wine. He hovers. 'Please, sit.'

He picks up her volume of Byron, flips a few pages, puts it down saying it seems so strange to read it in English, all the rhymes are wrong. She hopes he notices the *Archaeological Guide*.

She watches him more alertly now. But he drinks wine, smokes a cigarette and then says he must be going. They kiss three times on the cheek; she sees him to the door. '*Ciao*, Federico. *E grazie.*'

'*Prego. Piacere.*' He waves. '*Arrivederci.*'

✦

Suddenly she feels wonderful. Was it the cathartic trip home with Jack, or the joy of meeting people, or the pancakes she's been making for comfort? Her heart races when she wakes up.

Everything seems bright and crisp; the weather is sharp. She wants to bite into reality and chew it.

Of course she is a little abashed, after all the melodramatic emotion of New Year's Eve. Was Jack right: was she just bunging it on? It hadn't felt like it. It seems more like a seesaw, plunging her down so quickly; then soaring her aloft. She doesn't understand herself but, in this new mood of glory, self-analysis is unnecessary.

Guido rings her again. They haven't spoken since before New Year's Eve. She'd forgotten to tell him she wasn't coming to visit. 'Hey there.'

He too is in a good mood. 'I can't get you out of my mind. It makes me look stupid,' he says, 'but I love you.'

She laughs. 'No, you don't.'

'I do! I do!'

'Ah, Guido…' He admits that the first night they met, when she arrived at Hotel Fiamma, he had jerked off thinking of her.

'Oh.' How creepy. She supposes it's a compliment. She does feel a little violated but does it hurt? It was only the thought of her. 'Well. Thank you?'

'That is okay. And now tell me. Tell me a sexy story.'

She tells one from her working days, about how she had once made love to a man with eight of his friends watching.

'And they all come?'

'Yes. They all came, watching the two of us.' Now she is picturing the scene, two naked bodies plaited and bucking, a silent circle of men. There is something arousing about it. The reality was less wonderful.

He sighs, happy. She wonders if he's playing with himself. 'You're not jealous?' she says dryly.

'Why should I be? You are yourself. You like fucking. It's good. It's a good thing.'

How wonderful it is to hear that, even if it's not true. 'You're one of a kind, Guido.'

'*Scusa?*'

'You. There's no one like you.'

He is pleased. 'No. I am the only one. The only one who fucks you.'

She thinks of Jack. He too believes that. Now she is tired. 'I have to go, *caro*.'

'Take care of yourself. Be careful in Roma! Come and see me soon.'

She puts the phone down, and goes off to clear the pipes with a little masturbation.

✦

Jack rings her several times a day now, and sends texts in between. *Mate*, she types, *you are going soft*.

*Not possible*, he replies. *Man of steel.*

*You duffer*, she types, smiling. *I told you, I am not fooled.*

*More fool you!*

She is walking down the via Appia Antica, the old Roman road. It heads all the way south past Jack's house at the other end of the country. It is a brilliant Roman winter day, benevolent sunshine, crisp air. The trees on either side of the ancient road are burnished gold. She is amazed to find that only minutes into the walk she is surrounded by countryside. There are even sheep grazing in the fields. Under her feet flat paving stones are set like cupcakes in a tin, worn by thousands of feet, thousands of years. She feels young and bold with her big strides, heading towards the horizon.

The phone vibrates in her pocket. 'I was just thinking of you. I'm walking to your place.'

'Please tell me that's not true.'

'I'm on the right road. Should be there in three or four days.'

'Good grief.'

'It's a straight line. If we held tin cans to our ears and tied a string between them, we could talk just like this.'

'You sound happy. It's wonderful.'

She has learned that unhappiness does not draw him closer. 'I am.' They talk of walking, of the great walks they might take together one day, just the two of them, side by side, holding hands. She thinks of him pushing into her, flattening her into the ground; she stumbles as memory buckles through her. He tells her that things with them are good now. So good that if they moved up a notch he would be scared.

'Jack, I love you,' she says, 'dearly'. That last word saves them from crisis.

'I love you dearly too.'

Ah, how her silly heart glows.

+

Federico is walking her back to her flat—Tom is still away and she's glad of the company. They are old friends already. She is tired as they go up in the lift but offers him a glass of wine. When he leaves she kisses him on both cheeks, squeezes his arm.

Dinner is nearly ready when her phone sends out three little peals. She picks it up; Jack said he'd text when he got home.

*I want to make sex with you.*

Federico.

Her face creases with dismay. She stares at the phone, flushing hot. Oh no. No, no, *no*.

He has broken all the fucking rules.

She texts back. *Sorry. I don't want that. I like you as a friend.*

The answer: *Why not?*

She cannot bring herself to answer; she doesn't understand the fury she has to gulp down; she doesn't understand why this is a question she must answer, why she has no answer to it.

In the morning she texts Federico with an invitation for coffee. No reply. There never will be a reply.

She too, it seems, has broken a rule.

That night she dreams of an old boyfriend: that she tells him she is leaving him, and he turns to her with murder in his eyes and a knife in his hand.

✦

Tom is back. He opens the door and staggers in with his bags, bustles into the kitchen, cracks open a beer. The scales of solitude fall from her. Oh, their easy banter! 'Mate', 'Young lady', 'Cobber'. He asks what she's been up to.

'Nothing much.'

'Naturally, you little trollop,' he says, stubbing out a cigarette, and she can't tell if he's just joking or if he knows something; it doesn't matter, it's nice to be teased.

That night over dinner they open a second bottle of wine. They're talking about work: what it does for you, a sense of purpose, the gratification of accomplishment. She has breezed through a description of her wanderings in Rome—no mention of the farmhouse, a sketch of the streets of Naples—and Tom is looking at her as if she's spent the last month buffing her nails and slurping grapes.

'Have you ever worked a day in your life?'

She sits upright, half-empty glass in her hand. 'Of course I have.'

'Not a real job, though.' He knows she's gone to university; he knows she's worked in a bookshop; he believes she's a pampered puss with unblemished hands. He pushes her. 'You can't live your whole life depending on other people.' God, he thinks she's living here on some kind of allowance from her parents.

'I don't!' Another gulp of wine.

'You bloody do. You live in some airy-fairy world, all books and nice walks in the park and...'

She'll have to tell him. It'll be impossible to hide it. 'You sound like Jack.'

He doesn't say anything. A moment. 'Ah. So you've been down there?'

'Yes.' She is a little frightened, suddenly, but she says it. 'Yes, I've been seeing him.'

He pours more wine. 'Working out?'

Oh, how to answer that? 'He's a cool guy.'

'Whom you're fucking. Even though he's married.'

She makes a face.

'Anyone else?'

'What?'

'Are you fucking anyone else?'

Jesus. It must show in her body. A smile spreads across her face, uncontrollable. 'Maybe.'

He hesitates, then chuckles. 'You are a bloody trollop.'

'That's not fair. I really like Jack.'

'Yes, well.' They drink. They each look into the distance for a moment. They need a new subject. She can feel him watching her.

Ah, fuck it. 'Listen, you think I'm so useless, this princess. I know that's what it looks like. But I have to tell you, I'm having a rest. I've been working harder than you ever have, mate. For years.' Here we go again. 'I was a prostitute, back in Melbourne. I worked five, six, seven nights a week, twelve hours a night. I slaved. I had to keep my boyfriend and me together, pay the rent, pay everything; I never had any fun. I worked when I was well, I worked when I was sick, I worked fucking non-stop. Just so you know. I worked my arse off.'

'Literally.'

'Literally.' She laughs. 'Why do you think I have to eat so much gelati now? You saw me when I arrived. Skinny as a bone.'

'You looked fucking dreadful. I thought to myself, Who's this bloody waif? Looks like she'll fly off if someone farts.'

'I was horrid, wasn't I.' She is so relieved. So relieved. He's not fussed. He's making jokes. He's not rising to his feet and demanding she get her harlot self out of his flat. It's a mistake to underestimate people. She looks at him in apology. 'So now you know.'

'It still doesn't explain why you're so bad at mopping floors.'

'Hah hah.' She thinks of herself, coming home exhausted to sweep the floor of her house, plunge into books on the French Revolution and the Romantics. Taking off all the make-up. Getting up after five hours' sleep every day. The anaesthetic cream she used just to get through a night's work. 'I was good at it. I was bloody good and I, thank you very much, made people happy. Plus, I got paid shitloads.' She finds her finger planted on the table for emphasis. 'It was a good job. I liked it.'

'So much so that you've fled over here to pay your rent late and make my life a misery.'

'Yep.' She pours them both another glass. 'Sorry about the rent. Tomorrow.'

'Or you'll be hocking your arse around Termini to make it.'

She's about to protest when he winks, lights a cigarette, puffs smoke. 'Appreciate you telling me.'

'Oh.' She's embarrassed now. 'That's okay.'

'Well. Smoke?'

The second bottle of wine is emptied. Unsteadily she collects the glasses and takes them to the kitchen. When she comes back into the room he's standing there, his hands resting on the table.

'So. This begs a question. Why not me?'

She's drunk. What did he say?

'Why not me?'

This isn't happening. 'You're my mate.'

'Are you attracted to me?'

'You're my *mate*.' Please, please let him be teasing.

'A man gets lonely. Likes to cuddle. Likes to feel some female company from time to time. You're a lovely girl. We could be nice to each other.' He reaches to touch, puts his gentle hand on her arm. She can't bring herself to pull away; she simply edges into herself and the contact breaks. 'Come to bed with me.'

'I like you as a *friend*. You're my good mate. I...'

He looks down. 'Have you thought of me? Have you ever wondered?'

'I guess so. Yes,' she says, she had wondered and decided against it. He's attractive, but he is too strong. There is something in him that alarms her.

'Well then.' A glance so sweet, so unguarded, heartbreaking. He shouldn't be as drunk as she is; it's a disappointment.

'I have to go to bed,' she says desperately. 'I'll see you in the morning.'

'Come with me. Just for a cuddle. I want to hold you.'

And it is too hard, her thoughts are washing around like a bowl of water being jostled, she can't muster an argument, oh, a cuddle, what harm will it do? Her mouth is thick with wine as she says, 'We'll still be mates, won't we?'

And he says, 'Come on then.'

+

They lie in his flat bed and awkwardly fit their bodies into

81

an embrace. She already knows she has made a mistake. He cups her with his arms; strokes her body. As they undressed she didn't look at him; she doesn't want to see him naked; in the morning she will want to believe none of this happened. Her hand hesitates, skims down the length of his thigh. She is a knotted stomach in the centre of caressed limbs she doesn't believe in.

His mouth moves towards hers and automatically she turns to meet it. How hard his mouth is, how strong, too firm. Part of her is, of course, flattered. This great strong man wants her. But her body is dead, it is flinching into itself, withdraws from the kindness this man offers; she is crouching in the cage of his arms. In a minute she will make an excuse and flee to her own bed in the next room.

He murmurs, 'Oh, this is good, isn't it? It's good just to cuddle, to have some company.' It is as if he's become a different person: someone wanting, vulnerable, it is she who feels power now and he who is abject. If she were cruel she could despise him. She doesn't want to be cruel; she thinks, If this were Jack, wanting me so hopefully…Does it hurt me, to make him happy like this? But she can feel all the wrongness clashing in her head. It is like going to bed with an uncle. She cringes.

'See?' he says softly. 'Just cuddles.'

The wine sluices up through her; a kind of pity, too. 'Thank you,' she hears herself mumble. She falls asleep as quickly as she can. She dreams she is warning a prostitute about the police: they are on the street, with cars going past, and if she doesn't convince this woman she's in danger, they will both be caught.

In the morning he has gone to work and she wakes with a terrible sense of foreboding. She should never have done this. Oh, god, not again. What has she done?

She forces herself out into the drizzle; over the dog shit-smeared footpaths into town. She will walk the wrongness out of her. The surfaces of the stuccoed old walls seem to flatten in the drab light; the streets are stern corridors. Above her, lamplit rooms in old palazzi, timber-beamed ceilings, snug lives. Always on the outside, looking in. She walks in loops, nearing the edges of the old town and then swerving back in towards the core.

First Federico, then Tom. *Why not me?* This question. It is so monstrous, so unfair—her chest is full of heat. As if she's just spreading it around, spreading her legs, as if she's such a notorious slut she won't even notice one more man, as if he's entitled to a bit of the action, as if it won't mean anything to her, as if his envy and resentment of other men gives him moral leverage, as if—

As if she were cheap.

Is she?

A clammy awareness that, apart from anything else, she needs the room at Tom's. She's seen the newspaper ads: in expensive Rome people rent shifts in a single bed. There's nowhere else to go. Beneath the fury, dread.

Is she selling her body again, for a place to stay?

She has told herself that it will not hurt her, that it's no sacrifice. What conceit. Like some fucking angel of grace, some bestower of compassion. To these weak men who need her. These pesterers with their pricks. These losers.

Is it my fault, she thinks furiously, is it my fault I'm attractive to men? Should I stop being smart, being funny, being friendly? Having breasts and a vagina? Being an ex-hooker? Even if I wanted to, I couldn't. *Be proud of your body, be yourself.* I am being

83

myself and I'm getting nothing but fucked by these fuckers.

She will not apologise for being sexual. She will not be demeaned by accusations of promiscuity. She can't back down from her belief that she is entitled to sex, that her body, flawed as it is, deserves pleasure and admiration. That, indeed, she has pride.

And yet, that hand roughing her last night, her muted mouth, Guido's hand sliding beneath her bra, the feeling of being *handled*.

Chimpanzees all fuck the same female. When a female is on heat, they gather around, pricks pointing and ready. It's biology. Animals, she thinks scornfully, you're nothing but animals.

Through narrowed eyes she looks coldly at the men around her: their hairy wrists, their huge ears, the way they sit with legs insolently splayed, their sureness as they stride across the street. They seem a separate species. What must it be like to be one of these creatures? To have that bodily heft—to occupy that much space, so unapologetically—to be so ugly and expect everyone to love you nonetheless? Indeed, to applaud you? The world, still made for the comfort of middle-aged men.

As she walks, a man whistles at her; she bites her lip, hears him whistle again—no doubt at the next woman.

Maybe she likes middle-aged men because she can siphon a little of their prerogatives. She tries walking like a hefty man; stumbles immediately. Ridiculous. And, of course, they don't even know how much they assume, they have no clue. It would be funny if it weren't so pathetic.

A suspicion that she despises Tom for showing the same vulnerability she fears in herself. Well, it's his problem, not hers. At his age, surely she doesn't have to look after him.

And Jack. How he makes her feel at once desired and humiliated, and how he told her she was too good in bed, he didn't trust her. His cock sagging inside her, from fear.

She wishes she could respect a single one of these men who demand so much from her.

That night her heart jerks when Tom's key sounds in the lock. 'Hey.'

'Hey.' He goes into his room to change; the apartment is silent as she waits in the lounge. He goes to the kitchen; the sound of the fridge door opening. He enters carrying a beer. They both hesitate, then sit, as they usually do, and Tom turns on the TV to watch the news.

It is not until dinner is eaten that he says, 'I'm sorry if I made you uncomfortable. Last night.'

Oh. She was all ready for conflict. She wasn't expecting contrition. 'That's okay.'

'I thought we could make each other happy. I know you're finding your way here. I know it must be hard sometimes. You're a good chick.'

'Well, thank you.' She smiles. 'You're a good bloke.' Perhaps they can just skim over what happened; perhaps nothing has changed. Perhaps she saw a moral issue where there was only a man offering, and herself taking. Being with Jack has primed her for righteousness. But then she wonders if giving up anger is a sign of her weakness.

'I mean, just because you throw your legs open for half of Italy...' Fuck him, fuck him—but he's only teasing her. 'You can't blame me for wanting you.'

She had blamed him. The jibe hurts. But now he's so uncharacteristically softened, almost sheepish. There is wistfulness on his craggy face. He is no threat to her. He's her friend. It is she who feels contrite, for having judged and raged.

✦

Later, she slips out of her bed, wraps a blanket around her cold nakedness, goes to the unlit lounge and rings Jack.

'Is it too late? Are you asleep?'

'No.' His voice is deep from the hour of night. 'No. I was sitting here with the fire, thinking of you.'

'What were you thinking?' She is whispering in the dark, curled on the couch in her cocoon. She shivers, settles. 'Were you thinking of my breasts?'

'Mmm. I was. And your hips.'

'Were you thinking of my…skin?'

'I was thinking of your mouth on me.'

This strange sex they have, this fantasy of what they don't actually do anymore. It is comforting. She cups her hand over her pubis and snuggles down further in the couch, letting Jack's voice caress her. She is so grateful that she may have this pleasure and yet suffer no clumsy hand on her real, apprehensive, susceptible skin. It feels, for a moment, almost as safe as love.

part three

# MASSIMO

✦

*In short, I believe there is no honest man in the world who does not have some sort of expectation.*
**GIACOMO CASANOVA**

The next day she is back on the train, heading to Jack's but stopping for a couple of days in Naples—why not? She doesn't know which she is more excited about: finally seeing Jack again, after the tear-soaked farewell two weeks ago, or another venture to the mad world of Napoli. One thing is certain: she is glad to be leaving Rome for now. She's made calls, she's made plans. Her carriage is nearly empty and she lolls against the window, staring out sightless at the bright scrubby coast in a window-warmed daze.

Guido picks her up at the station and shows her to a car. It is a battered little blue thing. 'Wow,' she says. 'For me?' He leaps in front of it, strikes a pose, and beats his chest.

'My proud!'

She's laughing. 'Pride?'

'Yes.' He hops into the driver's seat. 'Yes, my proud. Pride. Beautiful like you.' Seatbelts undone, they zoom into the traffic. On all sides cars loom towards them, veer away; horns are sounded, men's voices shout, but the little car weaves into what seems to be a lane and lunges through the streets. 'So you have come to see me again.'

'How could I resist?' It's so exhilarating, this hyperactive man with his flashing white grin, his good humour and the twilight settling on the seething city. After Rome's magnificence, Naples seems human.

As they drive he tugs at his fly. 'I have a present for you,' he says.

'Oh my god.'

'In the back.' She looks: a box of chocolates. When she turns back, he has his penis out. A chortle. 'Maybe you can help me a little before…?'

'You're kidding. You Italians, you're so sleazy!'

He laughs. '*Non ho capito.*'

With a sigh she takes it in her hand, rubs clumsily. If he weren't so stupid and cute, this would be tiresome. 'Well. Thank you for the chocolates.'

Five minutes later Guido jerks the car to a halt outside a bar on the waterfront of Mergellina. To one side the bay smooths darkly. This road is weird in its glossy restaurants, their great glass windows and subtle lighting, so different to the ragged streets they've passed through. It reminds her of Melbourne; she steps inside the chic enoteca with a sense that reality has shifted. They have been sitting with a glass of wine for only a minute when two people walk towards them and Guido leaps to his feet. 'Katie, *ecco mio fratello*, Massimo. And…?'

'Allegra,' says the elegant young woman, extending her hand.

Guido was right, his brother is handsome. The same dazzling eyes in a tanned face, strong Naples bones. He is like a 1950s film star, all jut-jawed and suave in a rollneck jumper. '*Piacere,*' he says. 'It is my pleasure to meet you.'

Now it's all in Italian—Allegra doesn't speak English. 'She is shy,' says Massimo, squeezing her hand. The woman blushes with closed perfect lips.

She sits listening to them. Guido is lively, casting reassuring glances back at her while flirting with the beautiful Allegra. Massimo catches her eye, a slow glance. She smiles when they all smile, understanding the good humour if not the words. Next to the glamour of this beautiful couple she and Guido look a little shabby.

Massimo and Allegra rise. 'I hope to see you again,' he says as they take their leave. 'Watch out for my brother. He is *monello.*'

'*Monello?*'

'Naughty.' Massimo gives her a wink. '*Ciao.*'

Guido sits back. 'So. We go to dinner?'

'We go to dinner.'

After the meal he drives her not back to the hotel, but to a street between it and the station. He unlocks a small door set in one of the immense portals of Italian buildings, and she follows. Upstairs he switches on a light in the hall of what seems to be an apartment. 'This mine and Massimo's. Half office for his work, half to sleep. We were *bambini* here.' He shows her into a small bedroom. 'Here you sleep.'

He takes off his shoes. She is not surprised. He stands and kisses her. '*Allora,*' she says. 'So.'

His face is sweetened with feeling as they strip and lie down. After meeting the dashing Massimo, she is beginning to under-stand Guido's hyperactivity, his fragility. The younger brother. It can't be easy.

They are rolling on the bed, laughing; his fingers delve deep inside her and she gasps, stiffens. 'Oh you like? Wait. Close your eyes.' He reaches and opens a drawer next to the bed. '*Ecco!*' She opens her eyes and he is brandishing a black dildo.

'Good god.' She mimes horror. The thing is a foot long and as thick as her arm.

'You like?'

'I'm scared!'

'You will love it.' And she does. The feeling of being so utterly plugged is overwhelming; she lets him wield it inside her as she lies back and writhes. For those moments she has not a single thought, only body. It is like being possessed. In between gasps she peeps at him; his face is suffused with heat as he watches her. When he relents with the dildo and fucks her he hisses, 'I like to think of you. With other men. All other men, fucking you.'

'How many?' She's dazed and amused by everything.

'Many men…many men…and then you fuck me,' he whispers, and she agrees, absently, 'Yes, many men…' she says, and they continue plunging into each other's bodies until it's over and they fall asleep.

✦

She is woken by Guido placing a small plastic cup of coffee and a key on the sidedrawer. 'I go to work now,' he says smiling. He kisses her; she's embarrassed, all sleep-smeared, her mouth tastes terrible. 'I see you tonight. Come to the hotel. Have a good day. There is a shower.'

He is gone before she's properly awake; she sits up and sips the tepid espresso. No sugar. The room is ugly, with a wood-laminated bed and old synthetic yellow curtains. Ah, Italians. She tries to imagine Guido growing up here: this might have been his parents' room. God, it might even be his parents' bed.

There is a sound in the hallway. Guido, returning? But it is Massimo who appears in the doorway.

'Good morning.'

'Hello.' She clutches the blanket around her.

He props himself against the doorframe. 'Did you sleep well?'

He must know she has just woken up with his brother. 'Yes, thank you.' She feels terribly messy above the blanket, and terribly naked under it.

Massimo moves into the room. She stares at him, perplexed. 'Guido just left if you were looking for him. He's gone to work.' He rounds the end of the bed, stands against the wardrobe. He is wearing a different jumper today, and she can see his pectorals, smoothly defined under the wool. Isn't he going to leave?

'You look very nice like that,' he says, slowly grinning. Those blue, blue eyes. He is ridiculously handsome.

'You're ridiculously handsome,' she says.

'Yes?' He makes a show of preening. 'Well, that is nice of you to say.' He sits on the end of the bed and looks at her from under his brows. She pulls the blanket higher up towards her chin. 'Are you nervous? Don't you want me to be here?'

'It's okay. I'm just all messy. I should tell you,' she says, and meets his eyes, 'I'm not wearing any clothes under here.'

He puts one hand on her blanket-covered leg. 'I'll go if you like.'

But she is enjoying this: the way he is making such a deliberate show of being seductive; the gleam of his eyes; the scent of Guido still condensing on her body under the sheet. It is hardly real. I'm not afraid of you, she decides. You, she thinks, shifting her leg away from Massimo's hand, are going to play a game with me. I know this game.

He says, 'I'd like to tell you my life story.'

'Yes?' They each have the same smile of scepticism on their faces. 'Go on.'

'But first I must make myself comfortable.' He bends to take off his shoes.

'Of course.'

He strips off the jumper, his tight black T-shirt, his trousers. He is wearing, naturally, designer underwear. His body is just like his face: taut, brown, ideal, with the sleek padding of flesh over muscles that Italian men wear so exquisitely. They seem strong and yet you want to sink your fingers into their meat. Massimo slides under the covers next to her.

'First thing, I am very old,' he begins. 'I am forty.'

'Oh no,' she says. 'How did you get to be so antique?' The hairs of his leg are prickling against her. He is warm and smells of cologne. He has probably spent the night fucking Allegra but, unlike her, he has washed. His hand, moving down her belly, doesn't seem to mind. It is a very sure hand; a sexy hand. She wonders if Massimo passed Guido on the stairs as he came up; she is distracted by some expert caressing. God, that's good. 'You must have had a lot of sex, to look so young when you're really as old as forty.'

His mouth is just about to kiss hers; he gives her a diabolical smile. 'Yes.'

+

'I think you also made a lot of sex,' he says to her afterwards as he cradles her against the pillow. There are two dildos lying on the sheets; he had pulled out the black one—she snorted in recognition—and then another, pink. Her body feels exhausted, wrung out. They both light cigarettes. 'You like it.'

'I…' she says. 'I like sex.' It feels like a confession. 'You know I am friends with Guido.' A nod. 'I am also seeing another man.'

'Italiano?'

'No. English.'

'Ah.'

'So. Do you think I am—' What's the word for slut in Italian? '—a *puttana*?'

He laughs. '*Puttana*? No. Why? Because you like sex? I like sex.' A wolfish leer. 'For fun. To keep young. It is good for you.' He shrugs. 'If you are *puttana*, then I am *puttana* also.'

Oh god, it's so simple. He kisses her, another devilish grin.

'Now I must go out for a moment. But I come back *subito*.' He dresses; she watches his lean body with delight. He blows her another kiss and walks out; she hears the front door close.

For a moment she lies there, gloating. She has just fucked two brothers in the same bed. Ah, Naples!

As she washes in freezing water—there is no hot—she sees her face in the mirror. It is very young. Her pale skin, her smudged eyes, the swollen dazed look of having had two shattering orgasms, of having been kissed all over. She looks angelic. The very image of gleeful debauch. *Puttana*, she thinks, well, well. What would Tom—what would Jack—think of this? She scoffs into the mirror and goes to dress, feeling hilarious. Fuck them. Fuck those cranky old men—they wish.

Massimo returns half an hour later. He catches her in an embrace and asks if she will have lunch with him. They stride down the stairs, chatting; across the roads and down a side street into a dim taverna. Massimo greets the waiter in the slippery syllables of Napoletano dialect; there are poems written on the wall in pen in the same strange language. 'Poems to food,' Massimo tells her and she can just make out a word that might mean 'fish'. There's no menu; he orders for her. She's not really hungry.

'I am married,' he says to her through a mouthful of spaghetti.

'Uh-huh?' She is not surprised. 'Allegra...'

'Not Allegra. She is a beautiful girl. My wife is also beautiful. I am in love with her. God, I love her.'

'Allegra?'

'My wife. It is like...sick.'

'Sickness?'

'Like a bad thing.' His face is pained, sincere. 'We love each other too much. We are married when we were nineteen.

I love her like a sickness. No good. *Pazzo*.'

'I'm sorry. Is that love, then, or is it…madness? Good or bad?'

He sighs. 'Both. It is both. I will never leave her; she will never leave me. We make each other sick.'

'Does she—' Yes, damn it, she'll ask the question. 'Does your wife have affairs too?'

Massimo looks shocked. 'No.'

'You seem sure.'

'She loves me. She is not interested in other men.'

Inwardly, she rolls her eyes. 'But you…?'

'I have to. It keeps me, how you say, not-mad.'

'Lots of women?' Guido hadn't looked surprised to see Allegra.

'I love woman, I need them,' he says, and gives her that wicked grin. He knows exactly what it looks like, what effect it has, and he seems aware that she knows it is just a pose. She likes him immensely for this. 'Woman: you make men so happy.'

'Believe me, we don't always mean to,' she says.

Behind her a voice says something cheerful in the quick impenetrable dialect; Massimo stands, takes the hand of the man who has entered, kisses him on each cheek, and says, '*Ciao, bello*. Karty, this is my friend. Nanni.'

He is tall, broad-shouldered and has the goofy, bespectacled, large-nosed face of a sidekick. 'Hello, hello.' He sits between her and Massimo; crosses one long well-dressed leg over the other. 'Shit, I need pasta.'

He gives her an amused, friendly look. 'You'll never believe how *stressato* I am. I went to Cuba last week.' Next to him, Massimo is already giggling. Nanni is going to tell a story. 'Cuba! I never been. I go because my wife don't give me sex. Two weeks no sex: *madre di dio*,' he says, wiping his brow.

'I once had no sex for six months,' she offers.

A look of horror. He orders food then turns back. 'Six months. Six months. It kill me. Two weeks bad enough. I go to Cuba, to a club.'

'Swinger club,' Massimo puts in, face alight.

'The rule is, if you put shoes outside door like this, there two of you and you want company.' He holds his hands side by side. 'If you busy, like this.' He crosses them. 'I walk around the house. Every room, busy. One room, another room: everyone have sex but me. I am sweating. Finally, someone available, one shoe.'

'Wasn't your wife with you?' She is curious.

He ignores the question. 'I knock. No answer. I knock again—boom boom. Nothing. I open the door—*Get out! Out!*—I run away—no sex. The next day, I leave. On the plane, one day, home—terrible.'

Massimo is convulsed with laughter.

'Oh no.'

'So. No sex at home, no sex in Cuba.' He looks sad; a plate of glutinous melted cheese is put in front of him and he beams.

'Why doesn't your wife want to sleep with you?'

'I am ugly,' he says, grinning at her. 'Look at me so ugly. So I ask my friend Massimo to help.'

She looks at Massimo; Massimo looks at her, smiling. Nanni takes a huge forkful of food and bursts into laughter. 'If you like. Only if you like!'

Oh, these naughty boys. They have probably shared that same look since they were teenagers, she thinks. She glares at Massimo. 'You set me up.'

'You like men,' he says reasonably. 'Nanni is a good guy. We will have a nice time, you, me, him. If you want.'

How on earth has she arrived in this alternative reality? And yet she feels no outrage. This is fun. It is light and easy and she feels safe.

Nanni scoops a forkful of lumpy, congealing cheese towards her. 'Here, try.'

'Good god, no,' she says. It looks revolting. But she opens her mouth, obedient, and chews.

✦

Nanni peels off as they leave the taverna—'*A presto, bella*'—and saunters away. Massimo takes her arm and they return to the apartment. As they climb the stairs she feels they are already a companionable old couple. Massimo sweeps her around and into his arms. 'You like Nanni?'

'Yes.'

'You like me more?'

'Yes.'

'*Bene!*' he growls and pulls her giggling through to the bedroom.

She is lying on her back with Massimo's head between her legs when the key sounds in the lock. Fuck, don't let it be Guido. Oh god, Guido. But it is Nanni who stands in the doorway, looking shocked. 'You start without me! I tell you, I never get sex.'

Massimo's head appears from under the blanket. '*Ciao, bello,*' he says, and plucks a hair from his mouth. She waves. Nanni undresses, carefully draping his elegant suit on a chair. His rangy body is that of an athlete gone a little to plump; he sports an enormous erection. He waggles it at her. 'Hello.'

'Hello,' she says happily, and when he leaps into bed and opens his arms she wraps her own around him and takes his kiss greedily. He is a very good kisser. Massimo, between her legs still, is also a good kisser. She feels, as she stretches out, that

98

she is going to be getting top-shelf treatment; these men have practised; they like women; and when they call her *'principessa'*, she only lifts her chin in pleasure and says, 'Yes?'

They wrap her and turn her; she is filled mouth, cunt and arse. The black dildo comes out again; she shouts with laughter. As she sucks Nanni's cock with Massimo taking her from behind she feels a hand tenderly stroke her hair. The room grows hot; they giggle between grunts; she has never felt so cradled, so taken, so occupied. She knows her face is sweaty and flushed; that her cunt is slippery with juice and her mouth tastes of two men's cocks. It is all wonderful. She is sorry, but exhausted, when first Massimo clenches beneath her and then a minute later Nanni finishes in her mouth.

They unpeel, sit back panting. Nanni cups his stomach with a grimace.

'Too much sex?' she asks.

'Too much cheese.'

'You can't complain,' she says, and he snorts.

Massimo pushes back his damp hair, gorgeous as a soccer star. 'Everybody happy?'

They nod, catching their breath.

'Everybody for coffee?' he says. 'Everybody fuckoffy!' He bucks with laughter.

'Coffee,' she says. 'Coffee would be heaven. My god.' She tips over onto her side, dazed and replete. The winter day, she sees out the window, is already done; it's darkening outside.

'I go to the gym now,' Massimo says when he's dressed. 'You want a hot shower?'

'Oh, please.'

'Nanni gives us a lift,' he says. They take turns gravely to kiss her before Massimo ushers them out the door, all of them smiling like naughty children.

Nestled back into her crotch is Nanni; Massimo's legs wrap her from behind. 'Oh fucking yeah,' she breathes. Nanni kickstarts the motorbike and they're off.

They veer and charge through the traffic, the night air cold against her face. She is warmed front and back by her men. Naples is still out there; she'd almost forgotten. This delirious day, this mad day spent in bed. Only last night she was with Guido. Only yesterday morning she was in Rome. Oh man, she thinks, I've come a long way. The dark city is full of lights and people and they skim past rotting buildings, churches, portals. If there is ever a moment in her life she'd like filmed, this is it, as Nanni takes a corner and the three of them lean into the curve with perfect trust.

At the gym Massimo and Nanni direct her to the women's changing room; she showers, glad to sluice herself clean, sorry to lose the scent of her triumph. When she comes out to wait for them she will not let herself watch Massimo working out. It would be bad for his ego. She catches Nanni's knowing gaze from across the room, makes a face at him, and goes back to marvelling at the Italian women exercising in full make-up and jewellery.

When they finish Massimo kisses her farewell on the cheek and tells her that Nanni will drop her back at the apartment. 'I go home now, my beautiful,' he explains. 'My wife is waiting.' Oh, yes. 'Thank you,' and there it is, that look he used to seduce her only this morning. He is incorrigible. 'I see you tomorrow.'

'You with me, *principessa*,' says Nanni, and they get on the bike and twist through streets all the way back again.

By the time she and Nanni get to the apartment door she is

nearly staggering with fatigue. They walk in without speaking; she wonders if she feels shy, to be left alone with him, but of course not, it is Nanni. He takes off his suit jacket and kisses her.

'I think I'm too tired, mate,' she says.

'Me too. *Dio mio. Distrutto.*' They kiss again, caress. But he is hard. 'Oh, that is good.' She can't help it; she slides her hand over him and undoes his fly, sinks to her knees and takes him in her mouth. The insides of her lips are chafed and bruised but this is something she can do, to show how grateful she is for the kindness, for the fun, how safe they have made her feel. He gasps; she can feel his knees trembling. There is a tiny rip in the sinew beneath her tongue that pleases her.

When he's done he raises her to her feet. 'You kill me.'

'What a nice day,' she says. 'What a super dooper day.'

'I go home now. My wife is safe from me.' He makes a tiger face, growls. 'Sleep good, *bella*. We see each other again.'

She is sorry to see him go, to be left alone, but it is wonderful for the day to be over. She pulls the box of chocolates from her bag and eats some. In the kitchenette she finds a bottle of spirits; she pours a glass; the bitter reek of grappa. She wanders into the front room of the apartment and flicks on the light: it seems to be an office. There is a desk and filing cabinets. She sits at the desk, looks around. Picture albums on the shelf. She opens one.

Photos, faded and yellowing, of the family: the handsome father—so like Massimo—the demure dark-haired mother, at parties in the '70s. Young Massimo, cocky, bare-chested at the beach, his arm around a beautiful young woman. Older Massimo, suave in a suit at a party, just like his father. And young Guido, quiet, on the side wherever he appears: his huge eyes apprehensive, his smile wavering. Did he set her up with

Massimo? She has forgotten to go to the hotel to see him; already he seems a long time ago. Oh men, she thinks. Oh, me.

✦

She sleeps a long time, curled against the cold under the coarse blanket. Waking is a shock: she cannot remember, for long moments, where she is. Oh. Yesterday. The boys.

She is still lying there, too cold to get up, when Massimo walks in, carrying, just like Guido the morning before, a little cup of takeaway espresso, and a cornetto. '*Buon giorno, principessa*,' he says, flashes her a smile, bends to kiss her lips.

Just like the morning before, he sits on the bed as she drinks her coffee, but he keeps his clothes on. 'How you like yesterday?'

'I liked it very much, *molto, molto*,' she says. 'You know I did.'

'It's nice to see you happy. *Che bel sorriso…*' he strokes her lips as they curve. '*Un'avventura*, eh? For pleasure.'

'For pleasure,' she echoes. He is being careful, to make sure she understands. No analysis, no problems to be unknotted, no angst. Sex for its own sake, because it makes the body glow, moves the blood around, because it can be done. She can't help a little prodding, though. 'All okay with the wife?'

'Ah, *sì*, she was happy to see me when I come home. We make love all night.'

'You're bloody kidding.' She had slept like an athlete. 'God. You're a machine.'

He giggles and kisses her hand. 'I am a machine. Sex machine! Sex machine!' He licks his lips at her. Then he stands, still holding her hand and caressing the palm. He must go off somewhere, he is picking up a new car. 'A black BMW,' he says, gloating. 'From Germania.'

'Wow,' she says. She'd had the impression he's a small-time retailer of electrical supplies. This doesn't sound quite right. She will not ask questions.

'I take you for a drive sometime. When you are here again, you call me. Call me any time. I will miss you, Karty.'

The farewell is quick, friendly—as if they will see each other again soon or as if a small thing is now finished?—and she waves him off from her bed with a jaunty hand. Then buries her face beneath the covers to sniff the sheets.

✦

Within a few seconds of Jack picking up his phone she knows he is annoyed with her. She didn't call him yesterday; he was worried sick, knowing she was in horrible old Naples; really, she has no sense of responsibility; the very fact that she likes such a dirty dangerous place says a lot about her. 'Didn't you spare me a thought at all?'

'What are you, my mother?' She isn't laughing. It's all so serious and stiff and reproachful. No giggles, no leers. No dildos with Jack.

She is toying with herself beneath the covers as she listens to him droning on about how hard he's worked this week, how cold it is in his house, again his concern about her. All she really wants to say is that she'll get a train down there the next afternoon and let him know what time to pick her up from the station.

'I'm sorry,' she says.

'Well, I really just wanted to let you know: I don't think I can have you here this weekend. I've just got so much work, you wouldn't believe it. I don't want you to come down from Rome and have to spend the whole time amusing yourself. And I think my landlord is sniffing about; he'll know if you're here.

He and his son have been shooting sparrows in the fields around the house all week.'

He doesn't even apologise. It doesn't hurt. She thinks, Oh this is ridiculous. Everything is a cover for him, against her. It is immensely boring.

They hang up, him saying that he's sorry she can't come, her saying she's sorry too, neither of them really sorry at all.

She drains the cold last drops of coffee from the little plastic cup that Massimo brought her and gets out her diary. She writes about how Jack loves his little game, this push–pull struggle. He who says he doesn't play games. He wants to conserve his dignity by making her forfeit hers; he tests her boundaries and chastises her when she gives way. He seems obscurely satisfied when he is proved right about the limits of their relationship. When she protests he calls her 'immature'. It makes her feel better to identify all of this. She writes with her fingers cramping tight around the pen, from fury or cold, she cannot tell.

He rings back as she's polishing off an especially icy sentence.

'You can have ten minutes,' he announces. 'I'm on my way to a meeting.'

'Oh, hello. Don't let me keep you,' she says sweetly. 'I know you're busy, poor thing.'

'I am. Bloody hell, you have no idea how much work I have. It's a madhouse here.'

'Can't you delegate some of it? They make you do everything.'

'Well, I'm the manager. It's up to me. I have to lead by example. Even if it kills me.'

'It just seems so unfair, you work weekends, you work late at night—'

'I love my work. It's important.'

'Still, you say you're getting tired—'

'It has to be done. That's my responsibility.'

If this stupid conversation goes on much longer she'll clench the phone into pieces. 'You know,' she says, 'sometimes you can be kind of ungracious.'

A hesitation—or a silence? 'Can I? I don't think so.'

She says nothing.

He waits; then, 'I'm sorry. I know you worry about me. I worry about you. We're an odd couple, aren't we? You so idealistic, which drives me *mad*—' she can tell he's smiling, '—and me, well, I take my job seriously, it's a good job. Perhaps I'm idealistic too.'

'I keep telling you. You're a dreamer, you just don't like it.'

'Hah. I doubt that. You know what I think of your bloody poetry.'

'You're a terrible bluffer, Jack,' she says.

'I don't know what you're talking about.' And off they go again.

She is in the middle of a long, desperate sentence when he says, 'That's fifteen minutes. I've got to go.'

'This conversation's been a bit unfair, you know,' she says. 'Are you angry with me? Everything I say you contradict. Do you realise that? Every single thing.'

'You can rationalise it any way you want. I have to work.'

'Well, I guess I'll talk to you lat—'

'Got to go. I'll ring y—'

They are racing to hang up first.

'*Bye.*'

+

She is dressing after a freezing shower when her phone chirps. Bloody Jack, she thinks, yanking her jeans up over her hips. But when she opens the message it is from Tom.

*I'd like to see you. Off to London tomorrow 3 weeks.*

Well. She's not going further south, after all. Massimo is busy. She's a bit reluctant to face Guido just yet (oh god, Guido). She's so cold: she thinks of the heating in the flat in Rome, of the familiar streets, the couch.

She writes back: *Coming home this afternoon.*

Her stomach is yawning with hunger. There were only those biscuits for dinner last night. She is taking hold of a second cornetto in a bakery when the phone rings.

'G'day,' Tom says.

'Hello mate.' She can't wait; she takes a huge bite and speaks through pastry. 'How's things? So you're off?' It occurs to her that Tom is really going away again. Look what happened to her last time she was alone for weeks. She says sincerely, 'I'm sorry to hear that.'

'Yep. Meetings in London. Then I'm going skiing again. It's a bloody terrible life. So how are you going down there in Satan's city?'

'Good, good. Making mischief. Eating cake.'

He scoffs. 'Typical bloody Marie Antoinette. So, you'll be back before I go tomorrow?'

'I'll get a train as soon as I finish stuffing my face.'

'It'll be good to see you.'

Warning bells. 'You too. But listen. You know I really like you as a friend. So...' Never mind his finer feelings. Just to be sure. Her cunt is sore, she's tired, she just wants to sit on the couch with Tom and smoke cigarettes and talk about human rights. 'Just mates, okay?'

He says with dignity, 'You're a free agent.'

In other words, *you slut.*

The pastry sticks. 'I just can't. Please understand.'

He clears his throat. 'Got to go. Talk to you later.'

The phone hangs up.

She chews the pastry hard. Jesus. These men, sulky as children when their plans are pricked. She's dealt with men like this for so long. But that was different—in the old job she could remove herself from caring. These men she does care about, but they make it so hard. And yet, they're her only friends in this country. She absolutely doesn't want to ruin things with Tom. Where else would she live? Somehow she doesn't think the apartment here in Naples is an option.

She picks up her phone. *Don't think I should come to Rome tonight as I can't match your feelings and I would like to keep your friendship as it is.*

She is not afraid of love. She is not afraid to be romantic, to believe, to be enraptured. Jack and Tom are, they are so deadly afraid; so they mangle her heart, they crush it down into the shape of the ordinary; they look into her open arms and see only a trap. Or wish she'd open her legs instead.

Isn't it the greater challenge, to dare to love?

She knows that she feels pity for them. After the rage, there will be pity. For all of them, including herself.

The phone beeps. *Ok. Bye.*

Oh fuck him, *fuck* him.

✦

The city occupies her for a few hours but it's exhausting. The weather is colder than ever. A coffee in a café; walking; another coffee; she doesn't want to wander too far, she'll just have to come back.

Eventually she walks in the door of Hotel Fiamma. Things can't get much worse.

Guido looks up at the door's opening with a concierge smile. It grows uncertain when he sees her.

'Hey,' she says, and leans her arms on the high counter between them. '*Ciao.*'

'*Ciao.*' He isn't smiling now.

She should have rung him, at least. The last time she saw Guido was as he left the bed they'd fucked in. Yesterday morning. When everything seemed complicated, but only a hundredth as insane as it is now. For a start, now she's fucked his brother and his brother's friend. Now she's facing him. Now, quite likely, things are not cool.

He comes out from behind the desk, kisses her on both cheeks. His lips are cold. She takes a seat. Guido backs and stands against the counter. Behind, that storage cupboard where he took her against the wall. After his wife—for Massimo had mentioned, with his hand between her legs, that Guido is actually married—had visited. Oh, this is mad.

'Massimo, he try with you?' He asks it straight out. His eyes huge, like a child's. '*Sì?*'

She gazes at him. Doesn't he know for sure? Maybe he didn't set it up: maybe—oh Christ, this is worse than she thought. But she can't help a coy blush. 'Yes.'

He bites his lip and when he raises his face to her it hurts.

'Did I do something wrong?' she says. 'I don't know…the Italian way, you know; I don't know how you do things here—Italy, Naples. Did I get it wrong? I thought you—I mean, you have a girlfriend. Massimo is married. I didn't think it mattered.' He stares, unbearable. 'You told me you're not jealous.'

'You fuck Massimo.'

'Yes. But I thought the two of you—you share the apartment, don't you? You left, and he came up straight away. And I know he has lots of girls, he's very good at it. I just want fun,' she hears herself pleading. 'I just want to have fun, you said that was okay, that's what you want too.'

He moves to the desk.

'I'm sorry if I hurt you. Sorry if I got it wrong.'

He takes a key from a hook and hands it to her. She does feel awful. The way he looks like a child whose world has been smashed. 'Here. Room eight. Go up, wait for me.'

She takes it, obedient. It's not the same room as she had before, but it shares the ugly vintage décor, the sagging bed. The room is full of winter shadows.

She sits on the edge of the bed and waits.

Five minutes pass. The door opens, closes. Guido stands in front of her, opens his fly, pulls out his penis. He stands, silent. She can feel his eyes burning into her; she closes hers with hatred.

In the hard grey light she leans forward, takes it in her hand, opens her mouth.

Afterwards she does not look at him: she walks over to the little sink, spits as hard as she can, and stands there silently. She understands she has been punished. She understands that she will never forgive him.

'Do you think I am a *puttana*?' she says, looking at him finally.

He nods. 'Yes,' he says sadly. 'Yes, I think you are.'

She turns and spits again. The slime sits at the edge of the plughole; she turns on the tap, rinses it away.

+

'It is a game,' he says. 'You have to play the game.'

They are back on the horrid orange couch in the foyer, talking. She has decided to conceal her rage; she will keep it, a glowing coal, to warm herself on later. Oh, what a day this has been. She watches Guido's mouth, that agile merry mouth, now flattened with seriousness. He is leaning forward, explaining life to her. She will listen: why not? Perhaps he can explain it, for she is baffled.

'You have to learn to lie,' he says.

'Do I?' She sits back. Jack said the same: *Life is a game and you have to play it right.* But she doesn't have much respect for either man right now, or the way they change the rules. What is this: musical chairs? 'I don't want to. I don't like lies. I want things to be simple; yes, a game. But a game where no one has to lie. I don't want to be ashamed of what I do.'

'To protect yourself. To protect others. That is the most important thing.' There is something touching in his earnestness. He is no longer the silent figure who stood above her in room eight. 'You have a nice life. Exciting. You want to have adventures. So you must learn to lie a little bit.'

She does lie. She lies to Jack, she lies to Tom, she conceals from Guido that she fucked Nanni too, she hasn't told anyone at home anything at all. Isn't it to protect them all? They don't need to know; it would only hurt them further. None of them is hers, so she is none of theirs. But it sticks like the slime in her throat, to know that she must be a liar. She has done enough lying in the past; here, far away from that life, she thought she could find honesty again. It seems it is not possible. It is not allowed.

'I want to be free,' she says wistfully. 'Can't I just have fun?'

'But you have fun with other people. It is not fun for them if you hurt them.'

Is freedom fecklessness? Is it so selfish? She wants to throw off all the reproaches; to run away from these men who lecture her and tell her that she's got it wrong, again. Jesus. All she wants to do is fuck and laugh.

But is that all? She is so terribly lonely, too. She tries to remember why she even likes sex.

'If I am nice to someone,' she says, 'if I fuck them because I like them and they like me, why is that wrong?'

He shakes his head. 'Yes. I mean, no. I fuck you, I like you. Massimo fucks women. We all play the game. But careful, *cara*. You must protect yourself.'

'I mean, if I want to make someone else happy, by going to bed, I thought…I thought that was a good thing. A nice thing to do. Perhaps I should just not fuck anyone.'

He looks horrified. 'No, no. Just…not Massimo.'

'Okay. Not Massimo. Whatever.'

She stands up. She realises she doesn't know if she's allowed to stay at the apartment tonight. She didn't ask Massimo, and now she can't. 'Can I book a room here at the hotel?'

He looks at her with pity. 'You stay with me. Of course. You stay here tonight.'

She lifts her handbag over her shoulder to leave. 'Fine. Whatever you say.'

✦

She is exhausted as if from combat. All the men, with their faces in front of her, their words in her ear. This whole farrago— Jack, Federico, Guido, Tom and, god help her, Massimo and Nanni—has taken place in one week. When she counts it up like that she feels insane.

She reflects that Massimo and Nanni are the most enjoyable of them all, because they are the most simple. They offer, she gives, they enjoy and share. But Massimo is also the most elusive. She cannot allow herself to become attached to him; it would ruin the game. He and Nanni toss a ball in the air to her; she must toss it back or forfeit.

Guido is a romantic gone bad, she decides. He wounds in return. Soured by sex, warning grimly of dangers. She notes the example. His laughter was what drew her in the first place, but he isn't laughing now. Nor she. How contagious apprehension is.

And the others—the older men—it would be a triumph to conquer them, to release them from their fears. Those men are hard work. She hasn't come here for that. She doesn't know what she's here for.

Naples is ugly as she treads off into it again, barges across the busy roads. The footpaths are gobbed with spit and rubbish festers around the bins, flaps in the dry basins of fountains. The old city is mouldering and it stinks. Mendicants sell crap in crappy stalls, pestering passers-by and hunching into their jackets, unshaven faces under beanies. A scruffy town populated by criminals. The footpaths and buildings made of ash and cinders. *Motorini* thunder past, horns beep, always the intimation of sudden death. There is no quarter given for a weakling. She walks impatiently behind a group of fat matrons: she hates their sharp voices and their old-fashioned coiffures, the width of their behinds, their complacency. Above her the old palazzi crumble away as if time is running to an end here.

But she also sees the late sunlight cast on walls faded to the colour of dirty gems, hears someone practising piano in an upstairs room, notices a gathering of nuns wolfing down pastries at a café table and the waiter's wink, and palely remembers that if she weren't so tired, she might love this place again.

Another coffee, for stamina. She takes to the streets again: there is always a bit more of the city to find. Dead-ends turn her back or unexpectedly provide passage; there is an enchantment sometimes, so that streets seem to disappear behind her and the city leads her on, always further away, and then delivers her back to the centre. She finds her way to the gallery at Capodimonte and gazes at paintings of nymphs, goddesses and princesses. *Principessa*. They all have the same pliant face, the dark flashing eyes, flesh one wants to squeeze to the point of pain. Perhaps with the pearls threaded into their hair and the golden chains around their ankles they are all mistresses, one way or another. Mistresses or whores.

She comes down the hill back to the apartment in the early dark. Naples grows teeth at night: at this hour it seems the only women left are hookers huddling around bonfires lit in bins, their pimps lurking nearby. The women gaze at her listlessly; they are not even as hostile as the respectable women. She raises her eyebrow in greeting to one girl, cold in a thin denim jacket; is there a flicker of reply? It is too dark to tell.

Two hours later and she is drunk. The apartment, to which she's retreated, is freezing cold: she's under the covers with all her clothes on and a bottle of limoncello clutched in her hand, the fluorescent light above glaring. Next to her an ashtray is filling with grey flakes.

Casanova, in the part of his memoirs she's up to, has arrived in Naples, fallen in love with a young girl as she masturbated him for the pleasure of an impotent duke, decided to marry her and then realised she is his own illegitimate daughter, abandoned years before. He doesn't see, he reflects in his memoir, that it would be so terrible to marry a daughter; but he abstains, with regret, and seduces the mother again instead.

She adores Casanova but there are times when he makes her want to scream.

She'll hide out just a little longer—something in her is worried that Massimo will come through the door with another woman, thinking her gone. She knows she must get out of here but for now she curls her legs up, lights another cigarette, and takes a slug from the bottle. She is feeling rather dramatic.

The phone. '*Pronto?*'

'It's me,' says Jack's voice. 'What's with this "*pronto*"?'

'I'm just practising,' she tells him. 'Everything is much better in Italian. It's more expressive. You can shrug and wave your hands around, let all your feelings out, it's fun. You still don't know any Italian, you should try it.' Is she slurring? God, she didn't think she'd drunk so much. It's only seven p.m.

'I don't know about that,' he says. 'Where are you? Back in Rome?'

'No. I thought I'd stay here for another night.'

He won't know what to make of that. Can he have guessed that she's been with other men?

'I'm sorry you couldn't come down here. Honestly, the work has been terrible. But I miss you. I really miss you so much.'

Tears rise in her eyes. Dear Jack, with his boyish smile, the fire in the grate. It would be dark outside, the flames so warm. 'Do you?'

'Yes, I do. Are you all right?'

'I'm cold. And I'm tired. Cold and tired. I wish you were here, to hold me. I miss you. Can't you come over here?'

He sighs. 'If only. We have to be adult about this. I know it's hard, but we have to work with what we've got.'

'Oh shit. I'm so sick of that. I just want to lie in bed with you and hold you and be held and just, you know, be quiet, and be nice to each other. Something simple. Something really simple like that. I'm so cold…'

'Perhaps soon. The week after next I'm—'

'Too late. It'll be too late! I miss you now!' Is this her voice, ragged with urgency?

'I'm getting tired of being yelled at,' he says coldly. 'I don't enjoy being reproached for things I can't change.'

'What?'

'It seems that every time we have a conversation you shout

at me about how I don't do enough for you. Well, I'm sorry but I do as much as I can. It isn't easy, negotiating a relationship with a woman like you, who lives in another city, all these melodramatics. I have a landlord on my back and a very difficult job with people depending on me and then this, this constant demanding that I give you all my attention.' He is biting the words down the phone; his voice is shaking. She has started laughing, as the pitch of his fury rises. It's so out of the blue, so dramatic—so unlike Jack—where has this come from? 'I'm sick of being analysed, I'm sick of you refusing to take my advice. I don't know if it's worth the trouble. I simply don't.'

She holds her hand up, invisible to him. 'Jack, Jack. It's all okay.'

'No, it's not!' He is not to be stopped. 'You like me to be strong and stern for you, but when I am you roll over and show me your tears, begging me not to be so mean. It is impossible. You are a very disturbed young woman. You don't know what you want.'

'You're ungracious to make this all my problem.'

'Rubbish. I'm the most gracious man in the world,' he says. She hears him draw breath, then, 'God, I have to work.' He hangs up.

Slowly she takes the bottle of liqueur from the side of the bed and tips it to her mouth. She wipes her eyes, and slides down beneath the covers. It is terrible, this dying of the relationship, when it should be so simple.

+

She wakes to the pitiless glare of the light, her clothes too warm and heavy under the blankets. Past eleven. She isn't really drunk anymore, which is just as well: she has to walk the dark streets to the hotel.

The people lurking in the shadows watch her carefully but don't approach. She strides, fast and determined as she can. In a way she'd be grateful for something to happen. It would be nice to have an excuse to punch someone.

She makes it to the bright cubicle of the foyer, to Guido's wan smile. He is on duty but it's nearly midnight and he takes her up to a bedroom, turns on the lamp, watches her dump her bag and shrug off her coat. He doesn't ask if she's eaten. They undress and slip between the tightly tucked sheets.

The sex is silent, business-like. The air around them is freezing. She keeps her eyes open; she is watching how she fucks him, how she performs, because it is what she has to do, for this bed for a night, for safety. She doesn't even pretend to come.

He rolls off her when he's finished and they both stare at the ceiling. Then he turns the lamp off. They lie there like an old married couple and he says sleepily, 'If you still here on Monday, I invite my friends. Three men. You like that, yes?'

She says nothing but is aware of the space between their bodies, the exact amount of air. She turns away.

It is still dark when the last of the alcohol drains from her and she wakes. Guido is breathing on the other side of the bed. She is astonished to find herself here. Is she really? In a bed in a hotel in Naples, next to this man? What is she doing? For a panicked moment, she can barely remember who she is. A tiny figure under a great dark sky, surrounded by emptiness, a man sleeping beside her. She has fucked this man, his brother, his brother's friend: they come from a world she knows nothing of. Naples. She is in Naples. They do not know her; they've barely asked her a question about herself, her life in Australia. She has trusted herself to strangers. Jack will find out and dump her. Jack: she doesn't know him either, they've been acquainted for six weeks, and he's further away than ever. He hates her. Tom is leaving, Federico has let her down. Fuck. Fuck. She is so far from home.

In the dark she curls tighter and whimpers.

My god. She's been naked with these men. She's let them see her horrible body, her ordinary, ungainly, weak body. What did she think she was doing? Her belly, her unshaved legs. It all seemed joyous at the time, that carelessness. She has bared herself, ridden on top of men she didn't know, open-mouthed: the image of herself makes her whimper and curl again. How lonely, how desperate is she?

In another life, she was a girl who stripped naked without a qualm, who leapt laughing onto beds, who felt every moment of her power over men. She had learned to make a good act of it. She had studied the form of confidence; of appearing to give herself up, while taking what she wanted. She had been very good at this.

Would these men love that girl more? Of course they would. That's what she'd enjoyed with Massimo and Nanni—a return to such steely joyousness. Eager to please, easy to please. But she has been fighting, these past months in Italy, to be Kate again. To be herself. Pursuing honesty. Determining her own way. Trying to be true to the Romantic ideals of purity, of authentic feeling, of renegade self-will.

She has only made a fool of herself.

It's a year to the day since she got off the drugs. One year. Oh, to be stoned. She had to be strong when she was on them; how is it, then, that she's so fucking weak now? Isn't it meant to be better? Isn't she meant to have triumphed?

She feels defeated. Only defeated.

And sex. Sometimes she wonders if she even likes sex. What's it for? Why does she leap for it, like a dog for a bone? Most of the time she doesn't even come. It is pathology—and appetite for life. It is a reaction to stress. It is a supplication for affection. It is action, an action that counterfeits engagement between people. It is what she has to offer, as she has offered it to Guido tonight for shelter, as she'll pay it to Tom for accommodation. As she's tried to draw Jack to her for security.

Is that the horror: that she has made a slut of herself when she doesn't even like sex? That it is she who debases herself more than anyone?

Perhaps these Naples adventures have been just to spite Jack for his rejection. It was startling, to have him turn aside from her body; for a moment she was quite bemused. How poor she must be in charms that this seems her only currency and she degrades its rate by usage. But she has taken pride in refusing some; was that her judgment finally stirring? Or just making others feel the humiliation she dreads? Jack would call all of this 'over-analysing'. He would see her now, leaking tears into a hard hotel pillow, and think her melodramatic. But it is not melodrama, it is the fearfulness of recognition.

She wishes to be free, virtuous, brave, joyous. The men around her say she is needy, neurotic, manipulative, disingenuous, hurtful, promiscuous. She knows she is deceptive, duplicitous and cynical. Somewhere in all of this is a portrait. She thinks this; and buries her face in the pillow.

✢

Cold morning light. Guido kisses her goodbye on both cheeks and they embrace stiffly. She thanks him for letting her stay; he tells her to come back soon. They both know that she won't.

Tom should be gone by now but she makes herself wait until afternoon before she gets the train back to Rome, just to be sure. God, she's cold. She is so sick of being cold.

The train is full of young men on their way to military service. She baulks as she enters the carriage: she's the only woman on board. But they are nervous and courtly teenagers of the south, and they beckon her through. They smell of cologne and new cotton shirts, and sit as she does, gazing sadly out the window.

Jack texts her along the way: he is cheerful, droll, back to normal. He says they were just having a tiff and he might fly up to see her next weekend. That would be nice, she writes back. She is too exhausted to care. The only thing she really wants is pancakes.

By midnight, she has made pancakes, watched four hours of *BBC World*, and is lying on the couch trying to muster the energy to go to bed.

'Hello there, so are you back in civilisation?'

Shouldn't he be asleep? 'Back, fed. Bloody tired. How are you?'

'Okay. Tired too. Thinking about you.'

'Oh yes?'

'I was thinking.' A hesitation. 'That I can't accept my good fortune in finding someone I like as much as you. Because I don't really think I deserve something so good.'

She is startled: this is what she's been telling him for weeks. Now he admits it? She says nothing, waits.

'I get close and then I pull back. I don't quite know why. You are hard work but it's also me, I suppose.' She is warmed with the glow of his sympathy; it feels like a victory. 'For example, why am I ringing you at midnight when I should be asleep? This is how much I care. I worry about you. It's madness. Why we have these long phone calls I don't know.'

'Maybe because you enjoy talking to me?'

'Don't be snide.'

'No, I'm serious. You're the one who makes the call. It's something you should ask yourself.'

'That's it,' he says. 'That's what I'm trying to explain, though you refuse to listen.' And there they are, snapping back into an argument. 'I don't ask myself questions, I don't need to. I don't want to and in fact I don't want you asking them.'

'You asked me!' Oh *god*, not this whole pointless diatribe again. 'You're doing *what you just said*, getting close and then finding an excuse to pull back. Listen to yourself. You're doing it.'

'You know what I wish? I wish that we'd signed a contract at the very start, with boundaries marked.'

She exhales. 'That would suit you, would it? That's the kind of relationship you'd like?'

'It would stop you getting at me all the time, this endless criticism. The way you keep wanting something I can't give you...' He rants on, breathless, unstoppable. He is absolutely clear all the time, he says; it's her fault if she doesn't understand. She bites her fingers in frustration as she listens. 'And I'm married,' he says triumphantly.

'I *know* that.'

'I don't think you appreciate that I have responsibilities to other people...'

She endures his furious, measured voice for another minute. 'Listen,' she says loudly. 'You're getting angrier and angrier. I'm *not* trying to analyse you, just to understand. You're not making sense.'

Silence. A terrible, taut silence.

Then, 'Okay. I'll explain it in *English*—'

'Oh! *Fuck* you!' she shrieks. The phone springs out of her hand as she hurls it across the room. Sits there staring at the phone and shaking. Final proof that she is unstable, mad, dangerous. What bad manners. What dreadful colonial manners.

The phone isn't broken but it is silent. She stares at it. Get control, take control, don't prove him right. She swallows down adrenalin, waits ten minutes. Then she texts him.

*I'm sorry I hung up on you but I can't talk to you when you're like this. I don't need it. And I'm not being oversensitive.*

Time for a quick couple of slugs from the limoncello bottle before he rings back. Her heart jumps.

She puts the phone to her ear.

'Why don't we call it a day.' He sounds as if he's been doing the same as her: steadying his nerves for the showdown. 'I wanted to still be friends—but not after that message. I don't need recriminations. It's lost its freshness and I'm disappointed.' Lost its freshness. Like something from a supermarket.

It seems unbelievable that they are still talking. She feels as if the world has tilted, tipped her over the edge, left her falling in space. It is strangely peaceful, this falling. 'If that's what you really want. If you're sure there's nothing either of us can do. If you're sure you've behaved totally fairly and not out of hurt, pride, or bitterness, or fear, or anger...' For example.

'There's nothing I can do about your anger. It frightens me.'

'My anger. Well.' She has none left. This is so *dreary*. Oh, if he'd only shut up and go away. 'I'm disappointed too. I can see why you'd want to finish it up. I guess you wouldn't want anyone getting too close to you, after all, and your anger.'

'I'm not angry. I'm disappointed.'

'Okay.' She holds the little phone in her hand for a moment, weighs it, puts it back to her ear. 'Okay. Let's cool off.'

'Fine.'

'Fine.'

'*Bye.*'

Here it is. 'Bye.'

And it is done.

Lying in bed, she thinks that if they had talked much longer his madness would have convinced her: that *she* is unstable, crazy, dangerous. A liability. That he is perfectly reasonable and she is wrong. His certainty about himself is frightening. He is one of the saddest men she has ever known.

She goes to sleep, still falling into space, so tired she falls until morning and never knows it.

part four

# RUFUS

*Go thou to Rome,—at once the Paradise,*
*The grave, the city, and the wilderness...*
**SHELLEY**

The next day, she wakes to verbs sounding in her head: *toccare.*
Touch. *Trovare.* Find. They jumble out of the way and she
thinks: Jack. She thinks: It's over. She thinks: Thank god.

Then a wrench, at the bitterness of it all.

But she rises, and stands on the balcony, smoking a cigarette, holding her coffee. 'Well, fuck me,' she says aloud, and
hears her voice quite cheerful. 'And fuck you too, Jack, you
patronising old cunt.' She taps her ash off the balcony, watches
it fall into the sunny air and, smiling, goes inside to dress. She
has slept for twelve hours.

Out comes the diary. She makes her handwriting careful
and firm.

It seems superfluous to write about Jack. As if she hasn't
spent enough time on him already. But she is fastidious in
dissecting the final moments. She will rise, noble, reprieved,
accepting. She writes of the importance of emotional honesty.
She has learned a lesson about this from Jack. He is one more
step in her development. He taught her what self-belief means.
She regrets that his head turned away from his heart.

A memory of herself weeping in his car on the first day of
the year.

She hesitates to write the adventures in Naples. That
involved lies. Lies are not the kind of thing she is interested in
today.

Jack would rather use a terse euphemism; she wants to explain things as fully as possible. He wanted her to be smart; when she analysed, he thought she was a smart-arse.

*The problem with Romanticism is that it carries such momentum.*

She dots that final sentence, stubs out her cigarette.

✦

A week of serenity. She cleans the flat, she reads books on the couch, she takes walks. The January weather is fine, even warm in the sunshine; the breeze comes through the balcony door when she leaves it open. She buys yet another guidebook; this one directs her towards nooks and secrets, doorways leading onto hidden courtyards, cloisters of emptiness and sunshine held between pillars like sheets of gold dust.

Still no grief about the ending with Jack. She waits, as if for a headache following anaesthetic; nothing. He seems someone she had known once, a long time ago.

She is striding up the hill towards an afternoon of wandering when the phone rings. She checks the number in apprehension.

'Hey *bella*.'

'Hey *principessa*.'

It is Massimo and Nanni. They pass the phone between them, giggling, schoolboys in suits. 'Thank you for all the good times,' Massimo says. In the background Nanni says, 'You fix me right up.'

'All the girls,' Massimo says, 'say hello to me but I say *no*. No, I am all for you, Karty.'

'Liar!' After the past days' silence she didn't know she could laugh so loudly.

'No no, it is true. I am for you. Come back here. Come back. We miss you.'

'You miss fucking me?'

'No. Yes. I mean, yes, *certo*. I miss you Karty. But not just sex. You are our friend.'

Not everything is finished, then. Not everything is forfeit.

Late that afternoon she is in another café, diary out. Now she can write about Naples: the glee, the daring, the way Massimo's body had loosened as he came, how the veins on his forehead rose as he pumped into her. A voice at the next table says, 'Big day you're writing about?'

He is her age: the thick, hearty features of a farm boy. Dark red hair, deep saturnine voice. He cocks a sandy eyebrow at her. 'English?'

*'Australian.'*

'Cool,' he says, extending his hand. 'Hi. I'm Rufus.'

She likes this café because it's in a piazza populated by Eastern European migrants. The kids play soccer, the wives chat around the fountain, men stand shrugging with their hands in their pockets as they talk. The café is owned by an Algerian; the other customers are usually locals. She's a little annoyed to hear an American accent. 'You're obviously not a tourist,' Rufus says. 'Do you live here?'

'I do,' she says.

'Me too.' He jerks his thumb behind his head. 'Just around the corner. I'm a writer.'

'Oh. What are you writing?'

He's from Texas, he tells her, and he was a marine. Iraq. He has an apartment on via Cavour, he's working on a novel. 'Five hours a day. Then I come here and I have my coffee. Talk to people.'

*Pick up girls?* she wonders, but he doesn't seem to be flirting.

'Nice. I don't have a job. I just walk around.'

'Rome's the place for that. Beauty, elegy, sorrow, wonder. The centre of town, that's great. I love the centre. But the outskirts, too. I spend a lot of time in the outer 'burbs. That's where the real life is, the poverty, the crime. It's scary, all right. But it's part of Rome. Part of the love affair with Rome.'

He talks on, like this. Like a writer, she thinks. He asks her where her favourite places are.

'Um…I don't know. The Pantheon. The streets around Spagna?' Tourist places. Safe places.

'There's a piazza out near Tiburtina, really grimy, you know, you don't stay there after dark. Shit goes down. But it's got life, man, it's really got the feel of things happening, if you know what I mean? Not the dead old city, but life now in all its gunky glory. That's a cool place.'

She nods, chastened.

'Hey, you want to go for a proper drink? I know this great enoteca near Fiori.'

'Campo de' Fiori?'

'Yeah. It's down a little street, you have to know where it is to find it. You wanna come? I'd be happy to buy you a glass of wine and just chat for a time.'

Is this it? But he has stayed at his own table, a few feet away, instead of hastening to join hers. He is solid, calm. He watches her make the calculation. 'Okay. Why not?' She signals the waiter for the bill: watches for a hint that she's one in a line of Rufus's tourist-girl pick-ups. But the waiter doesn't flicker as she pays for her coffee and her new friend's.

They find the enoteca, in a street she's not sure she's ever been down. She thought she knew this part of the *centro*.

As with Federico, as with Penny, they talk about travelling, loneliness, exploration, testing oneself, despair. They compare notes on how long they've been away from home; neither mentions why they left in the first place. He speaks slowly, doesn't mind when she interrupts. He pays for the wine; they go to another place for dinner. She rarely eats a proper meal out in Italy, it's too expensive with the vegetables ordered separate from the meat and they frown if you don't order two courses. Rufus tells her it's all on him, it's a pleasure to have intelligent company. Again she glances at him with apprehension. He's perusing the menu but looking up he says, 'I bet you get hit on a lot.'

A rueful grin. 'A fair bit. They're not shy.' She doesn't want to discuss the recent catastrophe. 'The women won't talk to me and the men just want to buy me gelati, which is code for "Can I put my penis inside you?" Pretty cheap deal at three euro a gelato.'

He chuckles. 'I can imagine. That's part of the test, maybe, for you. Learning to say no to the wrong people, yes to the right ones. To just meet people, I mean, have encounters with other humans, find the gold in the dross. I've met some amazing characters here. And others who I think wanted to stab me, though I'm such a nice guy.'

'Do you get scared?'

'Yeah. Of course. I'm scared my novel is shit. I'm scared I'm wasting my time here and I should be home, as my old man wants, learning portfolio management or some fucking bull-shit. I wake up petrified in the night like everyone. But that's why it's a test. It doesn't count unless it hurts a bit, if you don't have to pay something for what you gain. Right?'

The waiter comes to take her order. At Rufus's suggestion she asks for steak and spinach and—a quick glance at Rufus to see if she's being extravagant—potatoes too. If he turns out to be a sleaze, at least it's more expensive than a gelato. 'That's what I think. Even if it hurts.' She wonders if her face tells her story, that she knows exactly what he is talking about, that she is not the meek young lady he might imagine her to be. Jack, telling her that her face had grown hard. 'I think you have to do the things that scare you most. But then...sometimes you do that and there was a good reason why it was scary: it's a bad thing. I don't know how you work out which is which.'

Yes, he is a reassuring person to be with. He *has* been in a war. 'Bad things happen. But they're for surviving, too. And hey,' he raises his glass, a yellow wine so beautiful it gleams, 'here we are.'

'*Eccoci qua*, indeed,' she says, raising her own.

✢

She lies on the couch, six storeys up, and considers the space below her, what might have been there once, the long-dead feet that walked where the ugly building's ground floor is now. Or further below. Ancient Rome is mostly metres below the surface. All over the city chambers open up beneath the street; there are passages and crannies one descends from into streets once open to the sky, now ceilinged with stone and asphalt. In those rooms, the rumble of overhead traffic makes a sound dim and insistent as time. She imagines the percussion in those chambers—some still forgotten, unknown, enclosed—sounds never imagined when those rooms were made. Motorbike ignition, tram bells, the clack of high heels, the whine of computers.

But that hidden place reaches up, too. In places you can feel the vacancy under what looks like solid ground. If you listen, you can hear your own world's echoes returning amplified through the fossilised cells of the past.

✢

It's not a mistake, she tells herself as she pushes the bell for Rufus's apartment next to the red lanterns of a Chinese restaurant. I need a friend. There's nothing wrong with having a friend. She'll die if he imagines she's coming on to him.

He opens the door. 'Hi. I was hoping you'd come by. That sure was a nice conversation the other night. It gave me some ideas for my novel.'

His place is tiny, crammed into the basement of a big palazzo, his rooms jumbled over a couple of levels like children's building blocks. He makes her a cup of tea. 'That's good,' she says in surprise. 'Italian milk always makes my tea taste funny. To be honest I never thought Americans drank tea. I thought it was always *cawfee*.'

'I hate to think I represent the whole American nation,' he says. 'Or that I'm letting it all down.'

He takes her out, after dark, across via Cavour and along a side passage, up the hump of the Esquiline. The hill is a sketchy place at night, he tells her. 'I've walked through here at night,' she makes a point of saying. 'The gypsies don't bother me.' In fact she has even dared feel a kind of comradeship with them: poor exiles wherever they go. She is not scared of poor people, only of malicious ones.

'Well, you won't mind the dog shit we might sit on then,' he says and guides her through the darkened park where people huddle around scattered bonfires. 'This is the real Rome, you know. The Esquilino. In the ancient days it was all palaces and villas and fountains. But they cut the water off, so everyone moved down to the river, and for a thousand years Rome had no water supply and this whole place was abandoned. And look,' he says, gesturing, 'it still is.' They approach a glow of light and below them is the Colosseum. It is gloriously floodlit, unreal, and from here, right above, massive enough to silence her.

'Nice, isn't it?'

'What a fantastic secret. What a fucking amazing place to

come.' She lights a cigarette, he does too, they smoke in silence, just looking down at the great impossible thing. 'Thanks.'

He pulls a bottle of wine from his satchel. 'I thought you might appreciate it. Here. We'll have to drink from the bottle but I promise I don't have cooties.'

'Cooties?'

'Ah, you don't want to know.'

'One of the many things I don't want to know, I guess,' she says, and takes a slug. 'I love knowing Rome, though. I love learning it.'

'Rome is always the lover that got away. It's the most beautiful, enchanting, bitchy, subtle, obvious place. She kisses you and she bites you and kisses you again. It's all there in front of you, but you'll never come to the end of the mysteries. There are always more secret places like this to find, that are just there in front of everyone, but that's her trick, she gives you so much you're blinded. She wraps her arms about your eyes and steals your heart and you don't mind at all. Elusive…and delusive.' He gulps wine, leans back on his elbows. 'The Whore of Babylon.'

'She's a beautiful whore.'

'She makes you pay,' Rufus winks, 'but damn, if she doesn't give good service.'

There's a silence while they each take another glug of wine. 'Typical man,' she says absently, still gazing below. 'You guys still think we're all virgins or whores. Perhaps we're paid because men are always trying to buy us.' She looks up—she hadn't meant to be sharp.

But he laughs. 'You're right. We're such lazy fucks. It makes it all simpler, you know? And we love things not to be our fault. I don't know why you women can't just take the blame for everything, it'd sort the world right the fuck out.'

'Selfish bitches,' she agrees.

'Little trollops.'

'Naggers.'

'Scarlet women.'

'Vagina dentata,' she pronounces. To his quizzical look: 'Toothed vagina. The fear that the cunt will eat your manhood. A very tiresome idea.'

'Cool,' he says, and mumbles the phrase under his breath. 'Definitely going in my novel.'

'Oh god, don't let me encourage you.' She passes him a cigarette. 'We're all such misogynists. Even women. Sometimes, I think, especially women.'

'Hey, I keep out of it.'

She wonders for the first time if Rufus is gay. The thought makes her like him more. 'We're scared of ourselves, I think. You know how we were talking about fear? Doing what scares us? I think what scares us most is maybe finding out we're not scared. Then you don't know where you are. Where the boundaries are. How to get home again.' She hears her voice trembling, and turns her head away in the dark.

His soft voice. 'In vino veritas?'

'Nah. I just...' She falls silent. Then, 'How do you know, Rufus? How do you know when you're fucking things up?'

'I think travelling, being away from home, really away, brings out a lot of stuff in us,' he says in his gentle deep voice. 'It makes the joy louder, and the despair burn more. You're high and you're low, fucking low. You don't know where the centre is anymore. You just have yourself and nothing around to calibrate from. It's normal to be freaked out. That's what you're here for.'

'I thought I was special.'

'That's your eighteenth-century Romantic sensibility talking, young lady,' he says, and passes the bottle. 'You're pretty special, but you're not alone. You just love dramatics.'

'I'm getting kind of sick of people telling me, every time I feel something, that I'm being melodramatic,' she says, and she's surprised by how vehement she sounds.

He isn't ruffled. 'Yeah, well, most people don't feel anything. It's fucking boring of them. We're special. Just look at us. Fucking cool.' He raises the bottle in cheers, drinks from it.

'We are,' she says, knowing they're mocking themselves, so glad to have someone to mock with. He passes the bottle with a bow. 'Here's to feeling,' he says. 'Here's to fucking up with feeling.'

She drinks deeply, in the orange haze of streetlights above the Colosseum that has stood there for two thousand years, through pillage, earthquakes, floods and revolutions, and she lets the dark wine wet all of her mouth. She is so thirsty, if she let herself she could drink the world.

✦

The January weather is crisp, the sky a blue enamelled lid over the city; all the surfaces are scratchy with detail in the sun. Some tourists wander, romantic couples hand in gloved hand, kissing in front of the monuments, taking snapshots of their blissful young faces against the ruin of ages. She watches them from her café tables, she orders in Italian, feels both excluded and proprietorial. This is her city, those unreally happy couples are only visitors.

One day she makes herself go into a shop in via del Corso, and tries a leather coat. 'You don't want fur?' the assistant says, holding up a coat furiously lined with rabbit.

'I can't afford it,' she says. 'I'll take this one. I need to get warm.'

'*Fa freddo*,' the assistant agrees. 'This one, not expensive. It make you look a *bella signorina, molto sportiva*.'

'No,' she says. 'Just the plain one, please.'

She and Rufus hang out, but she worries that she's crowding him when she turns up smiling at the café in the piazza. An obscure trepidation that, having found a friend so companionable, she might mess it up. Her wanderings take her to the other side of the city for the next few days. She reassembles herself, carapaced against the world, her gaze focused on the cobbles before her feet. She already knows where each little street will lead, but keeps walking them, hoping for a surprise. The shade is freezing.

She is growing fat, her scrawny body grown past leanness into disarray. Plumps of fat over her belly, under her breasts. Flesh weighing her down. Her body is stashing reserves after being starved. She looks at it, appalled, for she's never had so much body; it seems alien, alarming—where will it end, this weird profusion?—but eating comforts her. When she goes out, she's glad of the coat to hide her chaos.

How easily she is overcome; doubt and inertia and fear flood her. Again, now, she lies on the brown vinyl couch, unable to get the nerve—for it feels like courage—to go out. The sky contains rather than expands. She begins to wake each morning near tears.

In those waking moments she is taken by the past, and all its remorse. Is it Rome? Freud used the city as a metaphor for the psyche. It contains all ages, jumbled together, pasted and buried and salvaged; the city makes enchantment out of this dream of itself. After the empire, she reads, the citizens tore chunks from the ancient ruins, melted them for lime to glue remnants of temples and baths into new buildings. The city was dissolved to remake itself. Marble is made of deadness; tufa is solid ash. A city of ashes. When she manages to go out she leans her cheek against the glassy cold surface of a column in the porch of the

Pantheon, and listens to her breathing echo in the shell of her flattened ear.

Perhaps it would be best to leave for a bit. She contemplates going back to Melbourne. It seems a hard, brittle bubble of a world. She would have no idea who to be there now. She barely knows who she is here. Perhaps she should go home, and then return here anew. She could use herself to make the money, to have more money here so she can stay on, could become more complete. She'd have to become hard again; could she use that hardness to give herself the chance to soften more? But her body has lost its sureness, she can't imagine doing the old work again. It is too soon; what if she slipped, what if the old troubles slithered over her? If she lost what progress she's made? Her skin crawls. No, she mustn't go back yet.

But how will she survive? It is ridiculous: for every small thing attained, the price must be greater than the gain. Rufus had told her the price was worth it, and she agreed. And yet, she is running out of reserves.

So, on the road. But where—Pisa, Livorno, La Spezia, where Byron and the Shelleys trailed? That was always the plan. She imagines herself getting out of the train station in one of these towns, walking miles across unfamiliar terrain with her heavy bag to an unknown hotel, alone. Too fatiguing. She has lost her nerve. Tom will be back soon and she dreads it for no reason she can name.

She can't even get off the couch: agoraphobic, claustrophobic at the same time. Fuck you, fuck you, she says aloud. Oh god, you hopeless fucking malingerer. She is swept by gusts of grief that come and go like a winter wind. It is like something tearing away inside.

There are depressions on the inside of her arms, where scar tissue has shrunk away to make tiny hollows. They took bites out of her, those years. The holes are so small, for all that disappeared into them. They're sealed now; the damage is on the inside.

+

Out late one night, she finds herself at the bus stop outside Termini train station. The asphalt of the bus lanes glitters black with frost; she jams her hands in her pockets and hunches against the chill. There are not many people around but close by a brown-faced young man is eyeing her. She avoids his gaze; now he is at her elbow. '*Ciao.*' His breath makes a plume into her face.

'*Ciao.*' She looks away to see if a bus is coming.

'*Sei inglese?*'

'*Australiana.*'

'*Io sono algerino. Siamo tutti stranieri.*'

'Uh-huh.'

The city has many North Africans, their faces sharp and brown, their eye-teeth crossed. She's talked to a few here and there; they are easy to chat with, cranky with Italian laws, fluent in an absurd number of languages, furtive as they watch out for the police. Rome is stratified with its immigrants: apparently the Africans are all Senegalese, Arabs are all Algerian, there are no Indians, only Bangladeshis, and few Asians but Chinese. Each group has its niche: the Senegalese sell handbags and pirated DVDs, the Bangladeshis go from restaurant to restaurant with long-stemmed roses and cigarette lighters, except on rainy afternoons when the bouquets of flowers are replaced with umbrellas. The Algerians do henna tattoos in piazza Navona and sell drugs.

The young man introduces himself as Mustafa. His smile, with its crooked tooth, is charming. She relents, they chit-chat about the cold, Rome, he compliments her Italian, says he speaks six languages and works as a kitchen hand. Then he edges a little closer. '*Vuoi roba?*'

'*Scusa?*'

'*Droga. Cocaina, marijuana, eroina...*'

God. She's been thinking of it, in a dragging despair, half flinching, half wistful. To get stoned. Just once. Things are bad already, what would it matter? No fear here of slipping back too much; it's not as if she'd get into a scene.

She has watched the sullen men around the edges of this train station, their eyes following passers-by. They look like dealers do back at home, but here, who knows. She'd never have dared. 'Ah, *sì?*'

'*Come vuoi...*'

And she says yes. Fuck it, yes. A solvent to corrode the misery. She is all alone here on the other side of the world; no one will know. And if they did? She's so used to being misunderstood, she tells herself fiercely as she follows Mustafa, why not justify all they believe? Flaky, unstable, self-destructive. Yes, I fucking am.

It will be good to pierce her complacency; good to savage herself. Good, and familiar.

The buying is shabby: she's taken down a desolate road, to a tenement where black men sit on the front steps and the upstairs lights show naked bulbs in uncurtained windows. Mustafa leads her up, knocks on a door, says something in Arabic; she says '*No eroina, no eroina per favore,* I want *cocaina.*' The roomful of men glances at her, she hands over thirty euro and is handed a tiny bag of white powder. She hastens away. Already she feels dingy, cheated, absurd. She can sense the men laughing at her, stupid white bitch. She walks slowly, deliberately through the Esquiline area, past bonfires and shadows. She is at home here;

tonight she is returning to a place she knows.

Back at the apartment she spreads two lines on a magazine, hardly able to believe she's doing this. But it would be grappa and Ella otherwise, same as every night. She snorts the lines quickly, tasting the bitterness at the back of her throat, readies herself for coke's buzz. Snot runs down the back of her throat— this is rough stuff, all right—thirty euro for cocaine, stupid, she realises it can't possibly be—she swallows down nausea and goes to the bathroom to spit. In half an hour she understands that she's snorted baking powder and heroin. She'd panic but she's too sleepy. Thank god I don't know where to buy needles, she thinks as she lies miserably on the couch waiting it out in a sickly fug. Or I'd be dead. I'd be fucking dead on the couch and no one would even know.

In the morning she is relieved to wake alive, and appalled at what she did. Now she really is frightened by herself.

She showers, feeling hideous, and won't meet her own eyes in the mirror.

✦

Tom returns. She hasn't seen him since their text message détente two weeks ago. But he bustles in, tells her the kitchen floor is a disgrace and why isn't there anything in the fridge, takes her to the English pub for dinner. She lets him pay. He drinks three beers to her one.

There is a moment when he looks at her and she thinks: don't. 'Been keeping busy,' she says. 'Lots of books, reading, stuff you hate. Battling with that rude bitch at the supermarket. You know, my Italian is getting pretty competent.'

'Good.'

'You really should learn some. Since you live here and all.'

'I can ask for beer and the bill and where's the bloody toilet.

I don't need much more. Some of us have real jobs, you know,' he says, and she is so relieved, they are mates again. At home she brushes her teeth, goes to her room. When she shuts her door the clunk of it sounds very loud. She hears Tom go to his room, hears his door swing but not shut. He calls, 'Goodnight.' There is no further sound. She lets out her breath. 'Goodnight,' she calls back and tries not to think of him alone.

✦

What do you want? That's what she thinks when Jack rings her. She stares at his name as the phone vibrates and buzzes. Good grief. His face flashes into her mind: lean, sardonic, that grin. Her heart is pumping.

'Hello?'

'Hello.' A silence. He clears his throat. 'How are you? I thought I'd ring and see what you're up to. If you're still alive.'

'Yup.'

'I'm just the same. Not much news here.'

Oh, you have been there all this time, she thinks. In your little house among the olives. She imagines him, his solitary dinner at the big table—or perhaps in the kitchen—the fire, him sitting by it nursing a glass of wine.

'You like things simple, don't you, Jack.'

'I do.' A scoff. 'God knows I seem to have a perverse streak. I invite excitement into my life from time to time. But really, I'm just a boring old coot. In bed by eight, that kind of thing.'

Is he expecting sympathy? That old act of the curmudgeon, not quite so charming now. 'You should come to the big city some time. Get out of the fields. Put your hoe on the shelf.' But surely she's not inviting him. She is surprised by how nervous she sounds.

'Oh, some time I might. Work is busy. Well, you don't

want to hear about that. I'm snowed under. Usual series of catastrophes at the office, a total bloody mess.'

'You're very indispensable.'

Another awkward laugh. He is nervous too. 'I don't know about that.' A pause.

'I've been busy too. I walk every day for hours and hours. You'd be proud of me. Legs like a racehorse.'

'I'm sure.' Yes, think of my legs. Think of my body, my strong young body you gave up.

He says, 'Well, I'm glad you're keeping occupied. I was worried about you.' Were you, she thinks. 'I don't like to think of you languishing.'

'A bit,' she says honestly. 'But I'm okay now.'

'Good.'

'So. How's the house?'

'Fine.'

'And you're well?'

'I've been doing a bit of running. Got to keep the old body in shape.'

She imagines simply hanging up. 'Great.'

'Well. I shan't keep you. Just wanted to touch base. I didn't like how we ended things. That conversation…'

'Oh, well, I guess we were both tired. And angry.' Don't think I wasn't angry. 'It's okay, Jack. I think it was for the best.'

'Yes.' He takes a breath. 'I wish—'

'Oh Jack,' she says firmly, feeling the pleasure, 'don't let's start all that again.'

Again, a pause, one she enjoys more. She says, 'I'd better go. I'm meeting someone. This American guy, he's a writer.'

'Oh. You don't waste time,' he says.

'Nothing's going on,' she hears herself say quickly. Oh Kate, she thinks, every time you find an advantage you give it away. 'We're just friends.' Her latest favourite Italian word: *una stupidaggine*: a stupidness.

'Well, it's none of my business. Just take care of yourself. I'm glad you have a chum. I'll call you again. Take care, Kate.'

'You too, Jack.'

'Okay. Bye.'

'Bye. Bye.'

Thank god that's over.

+

'You might think of getting a job,' Tom says. 'What the bloody hell do you do all day?'

'I'm a student,' she tells him, blowing on her nails. 'A student of life.'

'Jesus Christ,' he says.

She calms herself with books about Rome, learns names, chronologies, lists of popes and emperors and noble families; stitches names to places and places to history. There is no comprehending Rome, but there is a pleasure in the details. The legend of one last forgotten obelisk, sleeping underground near the Pantheon; another of how Rome will fall the day her secret name is announced: *Roma* backwards, the word for *love*.

The fountain on one hill that catches words and releases them, a hundred years later, from a fountain on the other side of the city. She doesn't know what she'd say, if she spoke into that dark space. She imagines herself bending over it, screaming into the depths. But she has grown silent.

Stones that have witnessed empires become her friends; she doesn't touch them, disdains even to look at them in front of tourists, but that's how she knows they are hers. Times long ago and dramatic infatuate her. There is a great restfulness in this layering, a cushioning yielding as water.

The city itself is her skeleton; she can nest within, plump as a heart in a ribcage, and as hidden.

I'm not a wimp, she tells herself. I can walk around the station of Naples at night on my own. I can bring myself to another country on the far side of the world and learn the language and make friends. I can manage a dildo as big as my thigh, she thinks, and a woman at the next café table glances as she bursts into laughter.

She needs rest. She will allow herself rest. She has to learn how to let herself rest.

'Another day's exhausting toil?' Tom says, coming home at seven to find her on the couch.

'Shut up.'

She's fought so fiercely not to become hard, she understands how troubling softness is to other people.

'Ta,' she says, taking the beer from Tom's hand as she sprawls on the brown vinyl, and they raise their bottles. 'Chin chin.'

'Up your arse.'

'Quite.'

✦

The phone line crackles with noise. '*Principessa, principessa*, how are you? It is Nanni, your friend from Napoli.'

'Which Nanni?' she asks.

'Nanni with the big dick.'

'Sorry, I know lots of those.'

He chortles and she is instantly back in that crazy bedroom. '*Senti*, listen, I come to Roma tomorrow and I ask if you are free to drive with me to Napoli. Massimo like to see you. He ask me to call you.'

'Really?' She thinks for a second. 'Okay. Yes please. *Grazie.* You bad boys.'

The next afternoon he looms in the doorway of the flat. Same beautiful suit, same enormous nose and bashful grin. He puts his arms out and kisses her on both cheeks, then on the mouth. She's giggling against his lips. He pulls a condom from his pocket like a conjuror, raises his eyebrows. It seems odd somehow to have him here, in Tom's flat; in the grey daylight as they strip and lie on the clammy brown vinyl couch she feels awkward for all the laughter. But she presses her smiling face into his shoulder.

Nanni drives her to Naples and they talk all the way. She is shy to ask but he tells her that Massimo has missed her very much, they both have, they're crazy for girls but she is the most beautiful *principessa*.

'Oh, for goodness' sake, I know you say that to all of them,' she says, and enjoys the injured look he gives her before they both snicker.

Massimo picks her up from the apartment that evening. He opens the door with his key and leans against the lintel as she walks towards him. He raises an eyebrow. 'Am I beautiful?'

'Oh.' She pauses on her way to kiss his cheek, pulls back and looks him up and down gravely. He's in a jacket, white shirt and tie, with a scarf perfectly knotted around his brown throat, tan unbleached by winter. Surely he goes to a solarium. 'Well. Not as beautiful as me.' She pats her own messy hair, makes a moue.

'Not as beautiful as you, *principessa*,' he says and kisses her. 'Impossible.'

In the black BMW he drives fast but only half-concentrating on the chaotic swerve of traffic. He slips his hand onto her arm, massages her shoulder, cups her breast and mock-sighs in bliss. 'How was Nanni? He look after you?'

'He fucked me good and proper,' she says, smiling out the window as his hand works under her top before jerking away to deal with a tight turn of the wheel. 'Nice guy. So intelligent. Such a *big* cock.' She deliberately strokes his wrist, tickles the delicate underside. 'But not nearly as nice as you, Massimo, oh Massimo...' She looks at him coyly from under her lashes.

He preens, then bangs his hands on the steering wheel with laughter. 'No, no! No one is as good as me.'

'You're the best.'

'The best in the world. Listen, tomorrow night there is a party. A big party. You come, yes? Nanni comes too. You have a good time.'

'Ah, no, you'll just leave me and go off with all the beautiful girls.'

'I will.' He lunges over and kisses her; the force of it sucks the blood to her clitoris.

The car pulls into a side street. A young woman opens the door and gets into the back seat. 'You remember Allegra?'

Ah, no one had mentioned Allegra coming along. '*Ciao. Scusa, vuoi sederti*...um...?' She gestures to the front seat under her. No, no, says the other woman. *Non preoccuparti.* They smile at each other sincerely. It is not going to be a competition.

Massimo drives down to Mergellina, where Guido had taken her, where they'd met for the first time. They park and enter a big restaurant with a glass front. They sit in the window, one woman on either side of Massimo. She and Allegra keep catching each other's eye; Massimo's satisfaction is so adorable. She wonders if the other woman realises she has fucked her man, if she minds. She admires Allegra's long glossy black hair, immaculate make-up, delicate bones and expensive clothes. She is aware of her own short hair, perhaps it was a mistake. Maybe the Italian woman cannot imagine this scruffy foreigner being any competition. But I've made him come, she thinks to herself, I've made him laugh like a cat.

They all raise their glasses. 'Chin chin,' Massimo says. '*Salute*,' says Allegra. 'Absolutely,' she says.

Anyway, he's married. They are both mistresses. So where does jealousy fit into any of that?

'I like your suit,' she tells Massimo. She glances apologetically to Allegra. '*Scusa, cara, è più facile in inglese…*' The woman makes a quick gesture to say she doesn't mind her speaking English.

'I make my tie like so—' He pulls it askew. 'I know the girls you like that. Grrr.' He bares his teeth. 'Because I am so lucky, to have two beautiful woman.'

'Like James Bond,' she suggests.

'*Esatto*! My name Bond, Jame Bond. Everybody love me.' He is ridiculously pleased with himself.

They eat and drink and, a little tipsy, get back into the car. Massimo drives them up the hill to Posillipo, weaving around curves, the car purring and warm inside. She has let Allegra take the front seat this time. They park at a parapet that overlooks the diamante lights of the city and the black curve of bay. In the distance, Massimo points out, a great mass, only just darker than the sky: Vesuvius, biding.

They stand, Massimo's arms around each woman, pissed and happy. 'James Bond,' she says, and he bends to kiss her; then Allegra. All around them are couples, standing by the balustrade, arms around waists, kissing. She feels sexy and European and alight with pride to be here with these two beautiful people on a glittering night in Naples.

'You like her?' He whispers in her ear.

She darts her eyes at Allegra. 'Her?'

'Yes. She is beautiful, yes?'

'*Molto*. I mean, *molta*.'

'Shh.' He widens his eyes in warning. 'In English. She don't speak English.'

Allegra is standing still in Massimo's embrace, staring at the lights blurred in the cold air.

'She is in love with me,' Massimo murmurs. 'I love her too. I told you, I love my wife but Allegra, this girl, she is so beautiful…' He makes a 'what's a man to do' face. 'I don't like to hurt her.'

'She knows you're married?' She'd like to ask: She knows you're fucking me too?

'Of course. I am a naughty boy but I am honest.'

'And you want to keep seeing her?'

'Sì. And you. I am greedy, you know?' But he's not really laughing. He absently squeezes Allegra's waist; she offers him an understanding smile, then looks away again. 'I love you woman. I am not bad. I'm Jame Bond!' Teeth flash but he looks tired.

She feels sorry for him, eager to help him make it work, and protective of Allegra. She can't quite believe they're having this conversation in front of her, so intimate. The other woman is calm. But is there a tiny irrepressible curve at the edge of her lips? Some glance of comprehension?

'I think,' she says a little louder, 'you should be truthful with Alle—with her—and make sure she knows you love her no matter what happens. You're lucky to have her, she's gorgeous. You are naughty. But you're very good at it,' and she nips his ear and he laughs and Allegra laughs on the other side.

'Andiamo, ragazze,' he says, and they get back into the car.

In the front seat Massimo and Allegra hold hands as he drives back into town, they talk in dialect, its sibilant elisions and half-finished words a mystery to her; and she knows that they're discussing her now, but she cannot bring herself to mind.

She is here, she thinks, drowsy as a child in the back, to add spice; to put Allegra on notice; and vice versa. Oh, what a trickster he is. But this is the happiest she's felt in weeks. When the car pulls up at the apartment near the station and Massimo opens her door but Allegra stays put there is a jamming of dismay in her; then she eases through and kisses him warmly on each cheek, pinches his ear and whispers, 'Good luck.'

✦

Is Massimo palming her off on Nanni? The tall guy comes knocking on the door the next day. She's been out for breakfast after a freezing night's sleep, and returned. She couldn't think of anything in Naples she wanted to visit; she's here for the boys. Nanni says he's sorry, Massimo is busy but they don't want her to feel abandoned, so he'll take her out for lunch. He offers her his lopsided grin but she can tell he's embarrassed. She takes his arm and says she'd like lunch very much.

Nanni talks loudly, makes jokes as they order ('None of that horrible cheesy goo, thank you'), kisses his fingers rapturously when the pasta arrives; and then drops his voice. He gazes at the table. 'To tell true, Katie, I worry about Massimo. He is crazy. Crazy for girls.'

'He sure is,' she says.

'Yes.' He chews busily, then swallows. 'But this is not good. This is wrong. He tell you about the party?' He shakes his head. '*Un disastro.*'

'Why?' She thought it sounded fun, an Italian party. All her friends down here, music, inclusion.

He leans in. 'It is not a party like that. I am going. With my wife. Massimo is going—with his wife. Not Allegra. But he invite you, he invite Allegra—all the wifes—he is for trouble.'

'Shit.'

'I don't know what wrong with him. He tell me he took you to Boccanera in Mergellina last night—that is the biggest *ristorante* there, everybody see—he showing everybody. They know him. They know his *wife*. If his wife find out, she tell my wife, and then she find out about me too—' He is distressed. 'A bloody disaster.'

'God. I thought it was all okay.' She feels chilled. It is not nice to see jolly Nanni talking like this, to feel the flapping edges of a situation. She'd imagined that things were all arranged since time began. No: this is trouble. She imagines Massimo, now a tragic figure, swept by great winds, heedless of danger.

'He is making more risk now. I don't know what he wants. I'm sorry, Katie, that you are in the middle.' He sucks his lip, pensive.

'That's okay. It's not your fault.' She puts her hand on his arm. They look at each other, comrades now in a different way. 'So…this party? God. It sounds terrible.'

'I will not go. Too bad. A very bad idea. I stay at home with my wife, who will be—' He makes a cranky face, '—but I no want to see Massimo my friend in trouble.'

'I don't think I want to go either,' she says. A vision of Massimo's beautiful wife, raven-haired, screaming at her. Knives. Neapolitan melodrama. 'I think I won't go.'

'You stay at the apartment, maybe have fun. Not so nice for you but better I think than the *disastro*,' he says gloomily, and signals for the bill.

†

*A tragedy, not farce*, she writes in her diary. *I arrived in Act IV.*

She examines her conscience. God, she was nice last night, to wish the happy couple well. Massimo's delicious smile, Allegra's grace and sweetness. They would have looked amazing fucking, those bodies entwined. She is a little sorry she didn't see it; but relieved, too. A threesome with the exquisite Allegra—she thinks of her own lumpy body—would have been a bit *di troppo*.

149

But there is one thing: why is she here? Now there is a whole afternoon of waiting, before the party she won't go to, a night in the cold apartment: she has been inconvenienced, she thinks crossly. And it would be nice to talk to Massimo, to walk down the street with his arm around her. She likes him not just for the sex—*just* sex would be tedious—but the way they make each other laugh. She understands his way of showing off, and then making a joke of himself. He is a great joker. A tragic joker. She thinks of his eyes so sincere last night, confiding to her. She admits it: she is flattered still.

But he only makes love to her because she is naked and willing and female. Because she is there. 'Sucker player,' Massimo had said once. 'Soccer,' she corrected. 'Sucker!' he said gleefully, and perhaps he knew it all along.

✦

By the time Massimo and Allegra knock on the door that night she is lying on the bed staring at the ceiling in a stupor. She'd told Nanni to let Massimo know she wasn't coming; perhaps the message didn't get through. She didn't want to bother Massimo, in case he was busy. From the glowing looks on his and Allegra's faces, he had been. Absurdly, as she lets them into the apartment she thinks of offering to let them have the bed.

'*Ciao.*'

'*Ciao.*'

'*Ciao.*' Kisses all round. Allegra's perfumed cheek against her lips, the feel of expensive linen under her hands.

Is she meant to be jealous? Will it let down their spicy little game if she's not? She tries to feel resentment as they all wander into the bedroom. But she has never claimed Massimo for her own: she is content if there is only a part of him that remembers her.

Meekness or maturity? She can't be bothered deciding right now. '*Senti*, listen, sorry, I don't think I should come out.' She gestures to her clothes: the jeans and jumper she was wearing all afternoon. Better to pretend she simply isn't prepared for it. More tactful.

'Oh, no worry, come,' he says standing close to Allegra; but he looks a little conflicted. 'Come, come with us.'

Allegra says, '*Vieni*, Katie, *vieni*.'

Doubt. But perhaps she should lend Allegra support? Maybe the other woman doesn't know what she's getting into, or wants her company.

'*Sì*,' and it is settled, they go down to the car. But Massimo looks stressed as he ushers her into the back seat. He drives without holding anyone's hands. The city is busy at this hour. As they pass a piazza a group of young men bellow after them. 'They like my car,' Massimo says frowning, glancing back.

With a jerk they suddenly park. 'Karty,' Massimo says, 'I leave you here. I go to pick up my wife. I see you and Allegra later, at the party.'

Confused, she gets out of the car with the other woman; Massimo runs his hands through his hair in the mirror; they blow kisses at him as he drives away. Then, uncertain, she looks at Allegra. '*Vieni*,' the other woman says. She leads them into a bar. As they walk in the door Allegra slips her slim hand into hers, squeezes it for reassurance.

Inside, they are greeted by half a dozen young people, their cheerful faces lustrous in the mood lighting and candlelight, the gloss of black glass walls. This is a chic place, again more like Melbourne than Naples. *Ciao*s all round, Allegra introduces her to Gian-Roberto, Andrea, Franco, Angelina, Isabella, someone else; she shakes hands, puts an amenable expression on her face, tries to follow the rapid Italian.

'*Parli italiano?*' Gian-Roberto asks her.

'*Così così.*'

'*Allora. Tutti parlano inglese per Katie,*' he announces.

'Drink? You like champagne?' She thinks this guy is Franco. He has a little goatee and glasses under a prematurely balding forehead; it's nice to see that this type is universal. She remembers Federico; forgets him again.

'Yes?' Champagne will go to her head; but fuck knows she's going to need some support this evening. Across the group, one of the women winks at her and mimes drunken staggering with an astonished look on her face; she laughs too.

Champagne is brought on a tray, the liquid glinting with honey-coloured bubbles. They all stand, take a glass. '*Salute a tutti,*' someone cries and they all knock back their glasses. Skolling champagne? These Italians are hardcore. The alcohol rushes through her before the bubbles are gone from her tongue.

There is a long moment in the next hour when she feels embraced, exhilarated to be managing so well. They sit on leather stools. There is much happy shouting over the music, flicking gestures with hands, mouths stretching wide and exaggerated shrugs, waves of roared laughter. More and more champagne; she wonders apprehensively if she should offer to buy a round, but when she gets out her wallet Andrea shushes it away, shakes his head in mock severity. From time to time Allegra catches her eye to make sure she is all right; they exchange smiles like sisters.

'You must come with us to Capri in summer,' says Angelina, a loud girl with short hair and big protuberant eyes over a pinched mouth. She throws her arms over her head. 'We take the sun,' she says grandly. 'We all take the sun.'

'*Che begl'occhi,*' another girl says to her, and gazes admiringly. '*Beautiful* eyes.' The other women murmur agreement, a chorus of compliments.

The group soon forgets to speak English. She sits bathed in the rapids of dialect and when they burst into laughter she laughs too, catching the gaiety. She knows she will look foolish, if anyone notices, because they will know she doesn't understand and here she is laughing like an idiot, but it is hard not to, she's happy, it's the least she can do.

Then a song comes on and they all squeal and rise to their feet in a circle. As one they begin rocking their hips and twirling their arms. '*Balla, balla,*' they urge her. She is standing too, but she cannot dance. '*Balla*, Katie!' they call, happily twirling hands with each other. She stands there, stupid and stiff. A moment ago she was drunk enough for the delusion that she could understand what Andrea had been shouting at her over the music; now she feels terribly sober. If she moves her hips all her absurdity will become apparent; if she doesn't the same will happen. The beat of the music is almost irresistible, and she longs to but she cannot, will not, move. The others tactfully give up on encouraging her; they dance on happily; the song ends and they sit down, giving each other high-fives. Now she wishes the night were over.

'*Andiamo al party?*' she whispers to the panting Allegra.

'Oh.' She gestures to her mobile phone. '*Massimo mi ha chiamato. Pensa che sarebbe meglio che non andiamo noi. Dispiace*, Katie.'

'Oh no, *non mi dispiace.*' They're not going. What a relief. Soon she will be back in the cold apartment. Home. No, that's not right. Home isn't here. This is Naples. What's she doing in Naples, really? What's this all been about? Home is in Rome. No, that's not right, not really home. Melbourne? All her stuff in storage, that bubble world she can hardly believe in. Where is her home? Little tears spring to her eyes.

'*Piacere*, Katerina,' someone is saying and they are all standing to leave.

153

'Oh, *piacere*, Gian...' What was his name? '*Ciao*, Angelina, *ciao*, Isabella...'

She and Allegra are getting in a taxi. '*Ciao*...' She turns her head from the window. 'What nice people,' she sighs aloud. She hesitates, then says, '*Mi dispiace, che non hai visto Massimo*.' Allegra must be sad, to have been dumped for the night. Is this her first time with a married man? It is nice to feel protective: a thin runnel of nobility flushes through her.

'Ah no. *Mi chiamerà*.' The mobile phone held expectantly in her hand. She raises her fine eyebrows. Yes, perhaps this is the first time; she doesn't yet know to expect all the disappointments.

They embrace when the taxi stops outside the apartment; '*Grazie mille, veramente*,' she says, and squeezes the slender shoulders. '*Grazie* Allegra. *Riguardati bene*. Look after yourself.'

'I will,' Allegra says in English with a small coy smile, and they both cup their mouths over their hands in feigned shock.

'*Sogni d'oro*, sweet dreams,' they call to each other, and then she has the door unlocked and she is alone.

✦

The next day Massimo turns up. 'Hello honey, honey, my darling,' and kisses her on the lips. He looks better than last night. 'Come, I take you in my car.'

'Your beautiful car,' she says, and puts on her coat. 'Well, I am a *principessa*,' but the word already seems dated.

She says, 'Everything all right?' and he says, 'Yes.'

There's a silence for a moment. In the sleek car she's aware of her dumpy coat, her heavy boots nothing like what a lovely Italian woman would wear. Jack's voice: *Dress your age, a nice gold ring, give yourself credit for who you really are.* She presses her hands beneath her thighs and says in a mild tone, 'It can be hard with women.'

'*Madonna*,' he says, snorting. 'Crazy. *Pazzo.* I am *pazzo*, you know.'

'Well, you like it.'

'I like it, yes.' He shoots her an unreadable glance as he takes a corner. 'But I fall in love. That is like a disease. When I fall in love—' he says the phrase as one word, '—it is like a drug. I am in it *totalmente*, I am sick for it, no control. *Un disastro.* I make everything crazy.'

'Can't you…not do it?'

'Ah no. I must. I am made that way. In Italiano, we say *sono fatto così.* It is my curse. Maybe a *strega* put it me when I was *un bimbo*, baby.' He waggles his eyebrows. It is hard to resist the charm of his fancy, that he is helpless against philandering, an enchanted victim. Casanova redux. She thinks of herself: Guido's hand under her bra, how quickly she was seduced by Jack, by Massimo himself.

'We don't always understand ourselves, do we.'

A sigh. 'It help to talk to you, Karty. Honey, my honey. I tell you everything, I can't help it. You are a good friend.'

She blushes, pleased. 'We are the same, *amico*.' They exchange a look, considering, candid.

'I am afraid of love,' he says. 'It is trouble.'

She laughs. 'You are so old and you didn't know that?'

'How nasty you are. I am a young man.' He pushes out his chest, chuckles, then collapses again. 'You are a beautiful girl,' he says, and puts his hand on her knee. 'Not for sex, just for love.'

'Oh. I don't know how to take that.' Is he telling her, she wonders, that she's dumped?

He says, grinning, 'I fall in love for you!'

A smack to his arm. 'Oh yes?'

She knows he is daring her to fall for him. She wants him

to know that she doesn't judge him; she is his friend. And she'd like them to keep fucking. But she's damned if she's going to be *that* generous. That would spoil the game.

'You're not going to fall in love with me,' she says. 'You have too many women already. Plus, I'm not nice enough for you.'

'Are you a bad girl?'

'Very bad. I am a nasty, cynical girl. *Brutta*. You've seen me, I don't always shave my legs.'

He rolls his eyes. 'I like your body.'

'Tell me,' she says turning to him. 'You know all these beautiful perfect women. Like Allegra.' She can't resist mentioning the name; it'll do him good to have to remember reality for a moment. '*She* always shaves her legs, I'm sure. But you don't mind being with me. Don't you mind?'

'I like fucking you.' He is looking for a parking space now. 'You know, Karty, men like to look at beautiful girls, girls like Allegra. Nice to fuck too. But we like *woman*. We can look one thing, fuck another.'

She takes that hit; she'd asked for it. 'It seems to me that part of what we like about love is who we get to be. Who we're *allowed* to be, when someone loves us. Not always a person we like. I don't like the way I am with some men. But if I like who I am with someone, I like them more too. Is that a good thing, or…?' She notices they have parked.

'You want that we think you ugly, *bella*,' he says with his hand on the doorhandle, 'but we like you very much.'

Another hidden little restaurant; seafood, only one waiter in an old jumper and stained apron. The food is delicious, oil like honey on her tongue, salty and full of flavour. She has become proficient in various kinds of pasta now. Massimo chews briskly.

Women on his arm, hair flicked back, admired by all. But

she has seen him, seen the wrinkles at the corner of his eyes, the fatigue of a hopeless romantic. She looks at him; he meets her eye and smiles. She knows exactly what it is, to smile over fear.

Casanova: the trickster, the joker, with the heart that broke over and over again. *Tu oublieras aussi Henriette*, wrote one cast-off lover—his best—in the window with her diamond ring as he rode away. He found it, staying at the same inn years later, and wept.

She begins to talk to Massimo about regret. The corrosion of things she did in the past, at home, how she is troubled by them, wants to make amends; but they are gone now, passed, and anyway, she doesn't believe in regret.

'I don't want to have to be sorry. I just live my life, you know? It all seems like a good idea at the time. Who would do something they knew was really wrong? Don't we do only what we think is going to work out?' But she thinks of the drugs the other night, her sick remorse for having been so stupid, the many times she's done exactly what she knew she shouldn't. Yet isn't even that part of who she is?

'We do what best for us.'

'Oh. But that means…do you mean we're selfish? We have to be selfish?'

He looks into the distance. '*Non lo so*. I don't know. Yes, maybe. But with love for other people.'

'And love for ourselves. I think that's the hardest thing. To love yourself enough to…to forgive yourself. We are so good at being cruel to ourselves. Secretly. Or in our behaviour. We do everything we can to forget how horrible we are inside, to ourselves.'

'It is dangerous to look in,' he says. 'I prefer they look at me.'

'Too easy,' she says. 'Too easy.'

Do *not* fall in love with him, she scolds herself. That would be ridiculous. Especially now.

But his brown throat, his blue eyes. The way he cradled her in bed. *We miss you, principessa. Honey. My honey.*

She is someone's honey.

The waiter takes their plates. The table seems empty, with only wine glasses left. 'Massimo, I want to tell you something.' She expected saying this again would be hard but it's getting easier. It's information, not apology. 'I...In Melbourne, I did bad things, well, maybe not so bad, but...You know how I asked you, at the start, if I am a *puttana*? I was. I was a *puttana*. That's what I did for a job. I worked as a *prostituta*.'

He raises his eyebrows sympathetically. '*Sì*?'

'And I did drugs. I was a heroin addict.' She doesn't mean to, but she stares at the table. 'I have to think about all those things I did once and what they mean, why I did them. I don't think I was a bad person. I was an unhappy person. I made other people unhappy. And happy. I'm clean, by the way—' she says quickly. 'I have no diseases. Just so you know.'

'You...No one—' He mimes a slap.

'No. I was lucky. No one really hurt me. I hurt myself most.' She takes a sip from her wine. 'It was a good lesson. I'm trying to learn not to be so unhappy. I needed to do all that, I think, so I could be strong. I am very strong now, you know,' and she looks right at him. 'Very strong.'

He says nothing. Perhaps he had already guessed. They stare at each other. There is real pain in his eyes, for her or himself, she can't tell. They share an understanding; they look away.

'Everyone has a nature,' he says. 'We are born so, or so... *Siamo fatti così*.'

'I don't know.' Now she's tired. It is a hard conversation to have. 'But everyone has a demon. *Un diavolo.*' She is sorry for him; he is not, after all, as strong as she is.

'I hope your *diavolo* don't...' He fumbles for the word. 'You are a good girl, Karty. A good girl.'

She hadn't realised how much she needs to know that.

✦

On the way back he wends the car into a dank side street; they park outside what she realises, too late, is the back entrance to Hotel Fiamma. Of course, it's the family business. He gets out; she gestures that she'll stay in the car. She lights a cigarette and blows smoke out the window. Either his father is on the desk... or Guido. God. She is sleepy after the meal. The cigarette is stinking up the car; she opens the door just as Massimo and Guido walk out together.

Guido stares at her, as disconcerted as she. She throws away the cigarette, rises, walks over and kisses his cheek. '*Ciao.*'

Massimo's phone rings; '*Ciao bello,*' he says. 'It's Nanni,' he whispers sideways to her. She and Guido are still gazing at each other. She says weakly, 'I didn't know you were at work.'

'You visit Napoli.' It is a statement, not a question.

On the phone she can hear Massimo joshing Nanni. He is teasing him for ringing up to organise sex with her. She wonders if all these Naples men talk in her absence. Do they scorn and smirk? Do they compare notes? Do they despise her?

Massimo winks.

'Yes,' she says, thinking, This is all too weird, even for me.

She notices that Guido is shorter than his brother. Massimo is superb in his expensive woollen coat and scarf; Guido is in a zipped cardigan, dandruff on the shoulders. Same features as Massimo but skewed, more coarse. He seems small and dry and ignominious, his expression inscrutable. She cannot wait to get away from him.

Massimo closes his phone; snorts. 'Nanni ask after you,' he says. Can he feel the atmosphere? He must have done this on purpose. A lifetime of humiliating his younger brother. Guido lights a cigarette, ports in his palm like a sailor. It is a hunched gesture, furtive and protective. He looks at the ground, then at her; is there a sketch of yearning in his eyes?

'*Allora, andiamo principessa.*' They get back in the car. She is pliant as a gangster's moll. 'I take you home now.'

'Massimo,' she says as they drive away, 'What does Guido think of you fucking me?'

'Ah, he is okay. He has his wife. Enough trouble.'

Did you set it up with him, she wants to ask, did you arrange that morning when he left and you came up the stairs and got into my bed? How many women have you done this with? How stupid do you want me to feel?

She looks at him and says only, 'Oh, that's okay then.'

✦

But as they climb the stairs to the apartment she does ask. With a smile, as if it were all a great joke.

'*Cara*, before I sleep with you I ask Guido. He say is okay. So I come up, to see you again, ask if you like to fuck with me. You do; no problem.'

*Molto* fucking *interessante*, she thinks. Seeing how Guido was so injured and shocked. Room eight. The spit in the sink. God, this family is insane. 'He told me he didn't like it.'

'Guido always worries. All his life, he worries. He is not so good with girls. He has friends who bring him girls.' Those tense shoulders, that dry skin. How he'd exclaimed, 'My proud,' so happily when he picked her up at the station.

How he told her she had to learn to lie.

She looks at Massimo. 'He made me suck his cock in punishment.'

He laughs. 'Jealous. Guido always jealous of me. You suck my cock only if you want to.'

He goes into the office room of the apartment, switches on the desk lamp, picks up some papers, frowns. She lingers at the door. What is he doing now? He seems a different person from the one with tears in his eyes at the restaurant. Then he looks up at her, intent; he is suddenly a man, a body: he walks over to her swiftly and kisses her deep.

She buckles.

Taking her hand he leads her to a chair; pulls his pants open— all the time staring at her fiercely—places her hand on his cock, already hard and silken. He sits with legs wide, reaches up, pulls at her zip. Obedient, but meeting his eyes the whole time, she undresses: leaves on her g-string and her boots. He gives her his best diabolical grin, the one he's no doubt practised for years; she laughs back, sits astride him. She is *not* going to suck his cock. He bites her nipples hard and she looks down on his face with rapture. The hot wash of feeling rinses through her, she rocks on top of him, he puts his head back and she stares at his brown throat and then clenching her eyes shut and grinding into him she tries to come; for all her striving she can't quite—she fakes it so fiercely it almost feels real, she bucks and rears; she nips his ear as hard as she can and he thrusts up into her over and over and the vein on his forehead swells and he comes. Weakly he wreathes his arms about her waist. They pant, silent.

'It's nice to go slow and sweet sometimes,' she says wryly.

'*Sì.*'

There is a long moment when she can't decide whether she loves him or despises him.

They untangle. Now she feels silly and naked, the g-string straggling down her hip. If only this horrible apartment weren't lit by fluorescents. They make her skin look dead. She pulls her jeans on, already leaking into them. Massimo tousles her hair. Outside it's growing dark.

He takes the bottle of grappa from the desk drawer and pours them two small glasses.

'Massimo?'

'Yes, my honey?'

'Did you know I was a *puttana* before I told you?'

He pauses, takes a shot of grappa, puts the glass down. 'Guido told me. He want to know I use a condom.'

Ah. So he knew before she told him, they had discussed her. They had sat and discussed her, and the possibility that she might be dangerous. On the other hand, she is impressed that they are so careful. What does it mean, that he didn't use one just now? Why didn't she? Oh shit, she's stupid sometimes. She takes another tiny sip of her drink. It is oily and bitter.

'I like you, Karty. Not just for sex. Not just for love,' and he looks at her kindly. 'You just want to fuck and have fun, be a friend.' She likes herself for this too. 'You don't judge, you understand. You are a good friend.' Or is it a look of pity? For a dupe?

Being a good friend feels like second prize. Being just a fuck isn't any better. The harsh light is showing his wrinkles too: he is getting older. But free and easy, yep, that's her. She might be a fucking fool but at least she's an easy one.

'I take you to the *stazione* now? What time is your train?'

And so it seems her visit is over. It has been extremely instructive.

part five

# GABRIELE

*Oh could I feel as I have felt, or be what I have
  been,
Or weep as I could once have wept, o'er many a
  vanished scene*

**BYRON**

Rome draws her out as the weather warms. Days are sweet with breezes and the scent of flowers not yet bloomed. There are still oranges left on the trees in her favourite secret park.

Rufus opens his door with a blank look, and then a smile when he sees it is her. '*Ciao.*'

It's good to see his calm, freckled face, hear his deep voice as they walk out and he talks of slums, hanging out with gypsies, how he walked all the way from the suburb Aurelia, far to the west, back into town and the sun was rising over the city just as he got to St Peter's and, although he isn't religious, he knelt from weariness in the piazza just to give thanks to himself for finding such a moment of grace. He is fearless. It does her good to hear fearlessness. She borrows it from him when he mentions he's leaving Rome next week.

The two of them have an unspoken pact not to discuss the soggy matters of the heart. They've shared tales of passion and fury and despair, but not that. So she will not tell him of her Naples adventures, of how foolish Nanni turned out to be wise, and cheerful Guido bitter, and bold Massimo sad. She won't ask him whether she was right to be outraged at Federico, hateful to Jack. She won't tell him how every night she looks at Tom's door which won't ever quite close properly. She won't tell him how she's finding it hard to masturbate, as if her body has used up all its urgency. She won't ask him if she has been a fool to want love, to look for it in such awkward places. She says only, 'Oh, you know me, I've been having interesting times.'

Around them Rome darkens, lights come on, the Forum sinks into reverie. And they talk of dead emperors, and labyrinths, and beggars, and grace.

✦

On a strangely warm evening, sweating in her leather coat and conscious of a pimple on her chin, she is walking in the city. There are many people about in the twilight and an excited impression of summer visiting in the soft February air. Around and around the old centre she goes, loving her favourite turns, looking out for something new. It is Carnevale; Goethe, she remembers, wrote of the festival two hundred years ago as a riot, furious and outrageous almost beyond belief. Now the only signs are children in polyester fancy dress and scatterings of soggy confetti wherever she goes. As she heads towards the church of Sant'Ignazio a young man stops her.

'*Scusa, ma sai dov'è Campo de' Fiori?*'

She pauses. '*Allora. Sempre diritto, attraverso Corso Emmanuele, è grande.* You can't miss it.' She is always being stopped for directions these days: a small point of pride. Perhaps it's her coat.

He smiles. 'You speak Italian,' he says in that language. 'Are you English? I don't speak English.'

'*Australiana,*' she says warily, because this question and answer routine are customary and, unless she's firm, no matter how cold the weather, will end in an invitation for ice-cream. She stops him as he starts to say, 'Ah, *canguro,*' making boxing-kangaroo motions. 'Excuse me, I'm in a rush.'

'Where are you going?'

She is about to walk away. 'Church.'

'Can I come?'

He's not so young, perhaps her own age. A grey suit and nice shirt, slightly balding curly hair, a merry broad face. He holds out his hand. 'Gabriele.'

She sighs. 'I'm going to a music concert.' It's just the proforma of an Italian male. A kind of courtesy. Perhaps he's sorry for her, sweating pimple-girl in a city full of beauties. She shakes his hand perfunctorily.

'*Bene*. I'll come with you.'

'It might be boring.'

'May I come?' A crossed tooth makes his smile wicked, even if he doesn't mean it.

She rolls her eyes. 'Suit yourself. But I'm going home after. No gelato.'

'*Va bene.*'

They take seats in a pew under a ceiling so hectically decorated with fresco, gilt and stucco it makes her giggle. Gabriele cranes to look at it. '*Bellissimo*,' he breathes.

'Ugly,' she says.

He pulls out a bottle of water and a plastic cup. She looks at him askance: can you drink water in church? But he has knelt and genuflected at the entrance; she supposes he knows what he's doing. He offers her a drink; she sips at it, hands the cup back with thanks.

The music starts: a gospel choir from the United States. They launch into 'Swing Low, Sweet Chariot' in full gusto. She imagines that they are thrilled, these mid-western matrons, to be standing here bellowing into a church four hundred years old, riotous with frescoes, strewn with golden angels. She listens and looks with sympathy but the music, after an arresting start, becomes cloying and sentimental. All that yelling about God. It's embarrassing.

The Italian is peeping at her from the corner of his eye, a

small smile at the edge of his lips. She catches him; he makes a show of staring at the stage. She sighs, crosses her legs the other way, concentrates on the swaying women in front. He is awfully cute, with his green eyes flecked with hazel and his smile like a mischievous faun. He smells of cologne; the suit is a little overdressed for a stroll in town. Wasn't he going to Campo de' Fiori? Ah, these young guys. Always hoping to get their end in.

Staring straight ahead, he reaches his hand to hold hers. Amused, she lets him. Oh, what's the harm? He'll feel better for having held a girl's hand and she'll get rid of him after this. His hand is warm and dry, short-palmed, calloused at the fingertips. Worker's hand, dandy's suit. She checks his face; he turns to her, smiles beautifully, puts his finger to his lips and gazes at the stage.

At the interval the church stops ringing with voices. 'What do you think?' the young man asks.

'It's pretty bad.'

'Beautiful.'

'Really? I think I might go. I've got to get home. Didn't you want to go to the Campo? Or,' she can't be bothered pretending, 'was that just a line to get my attention?'

He blushes. 'I really did want to find the Campo. I've been in Rome only a week.'

'Where are you from?'

And he says, 'Napoli.'

She can't help it; she laughs. 'Napoletano? Oh my god.'

'What?' He is laughing too.

'I know you guys. You're all *monelli*. You're crazy.'

'Perhaps a bit. But we are good guys too. Are you scared of Napoli?'

'Not a bit.' She stands and swings her bag over her shoulder.

'I've been there many times. I have lots of friends in Napoli.'

'Ah. Then you like pizza.'

'Yes. I like pizza.'

'Let me buy you pizza. For the concert. For the beautiful music.'

She walked into that one, all right. 'The music wasn't so good. I have to go home.'

'Come on.' The droll smile, the hand half-reaching for hers, the way he's looking at her as if he knows what she's thinking and he's not troubled by it. 'A pizza. It would be my pleasure.'

She makes him wait while she considers. 'Just a pizza. Then you're on your own.'

They stroll out of the church and it's grown dark, the street lamps sulfurous on the ochre buildings. They turn into the street behind and find themselves in a cavalcade of tourists and a melee of gingham tablecloths. 'Ach. *Turisti*,' she says.

He walks beside her. 'You're not a tourist?'

'I live here.' They're still the most wonderful words. 'What are you doing in Rome?'

'I am a...' he uses a word she doesn't know. He gestures, tries again; she understands he is some kind of furniture-maker. He has come to Rome with several other Neapolitan men for work; they live in an outer suburb in a shared house. That explains the roughened hands. That explains the careful suit.

'And you're out on your own tonight?'

That innocent smile. 'Yes. On my own. I wanted to see Rome. I haven't had time yet. Beautiful, beautiful Rome.'

'Watch out, she'll eat you up. A nice young boy like you.'

They're walking through the crowds, her via del Corso leather coat and the young man in the suit beside her; they look just like a thousand other couples strolling around. They have crossed busy corso Vittorio Emmanuele and are into the nook of the city near the Campo, its spellbinding little streets, its gelati-licking crowds. He is the Italian but it is she who knows where she's going.

They manage to find a modest pizzeria and order pizzas. They come, huge thin circles moist with cheese and tomato sauce. 'Pizza napoletana,' he says with pride. 'The best. Simple but good.' He makes an odd gesture, as if turning a screw in his cheek. '*Buon appetito.*'

'*Buon appetito.*'

They eat messily, folding the slices and shoving them into their mouths, cheesy oil dripping down their wrists. What does she care what this guy thinks of her manners? Gabriele puts a slice of his pizza on her plate. 'Oh, no thanks,' she says, and he puts another. 'No, really!' Another, all of his pizza. She finds herself guffawing through a mouthful of dough. There is something in the crinkle of his eyes that reminds her of Massimo. He's charming.

Afterwards they walk to piazza Farnese with its floodlit fountains spilling into Roman baths, the great Michelangelo palace as backdrop, people sitting at small round café tables looking out as if waiting for a stage show. It's still quite warm. Around the fountain couples are embracing and everyone looks glorious in the lighting. All of Rome, it feels, is a romance. Oh wonderful city, she thinks, what an enchantment you are.

They are talking about books. He likes men's health magazines. She says, 'I love poetry,' he cocks an eyebrow and she hears herself declaiming Shelley:

He has outsoared the shadow of our night
Envy and calumny and hate and pain...

Can touch him not, and torture not again...

Surely she isn't drunk after one glass of cheap wine? She is trying to remember the next line as they wander towards one of the fountains. He puts his hand on her shoulder, turns her around.

His mouth is there: they kiss. His mouth tastes clean, of iron and water.

She is already grinning as she pulls away. 'Oh my god. *Monello.*'

'Yes,' he says, and they kiss again.

'Bloody hell,' she says in English. 'You're fucking good.'

'*Scusa?*'

'Nothing.'

He is pulling her, laughing now, by the hand into a dark little street off the piazza. They tussle, reaching for each other as they half-run, giggling, stupid with surprise. He pushes her backwards against the bonnet of a parked car; his face is serious with desire. It undoes her; she stares at him. Two strong arms lift and place her.

'Are you sure this is okay?' She looks down at the little silver car she's sitting on. Under her she can hear the metal groan from the weight.

He pushes her backwards. He is between her legs, lying over her body, kissing her rapturously. She kisses back, but she's aware of the metal creaking; she starts to chuckle. He pulls back, looks at her to see what the sound is, grins and dives again to silence her. The hardness of him against her groin, a stiff stick of want. The momentum of his desire has her flat on her back; it's all she can do to crane her head up and push her tongue into his mouth, use her hands to claw him down to her.

'Hey!'

They're leaping off the car before they know it. Her clothes are dishevelled; frantically she pulls her shirt down, starts helplessly to laugh. A man stands nearby, staring at them. 'What are you doing?'

Gabriele's erection is mercifully hidden by shadows. He looks flustered. 'Nothing. Sorry, we were just—'

'What the fuck have you done to my car?' He comes over; they all stare at a bum-shaped hollow in the glossy bonnet.

She is trying not to laugh but Gabriele, she sees, is crimson with panic. She decides that she'll let him handle this. After all, it was his idea to ravish her on top of someone else's car. She's just the foreigner, she speaka no Italiano. She hunches into her coat, withdraws a little, watches Gabriele as he goes through the humiliation of agreeing to pay for the damage, proffering his identity papers, apologising, apologising. He is probably worried that he looks stupid now, she thinks, but in fact I like him more.

The indignity over, they walk away in silence. 'I'll help pay,' she says in pity.

'No no,' he says.

'Yes.'

'No.' They are walking fast. 'No, I will pay,' he says, and turns his face to her, elated. His kisses are like a devouring, but he never bruises her, never knocks teeth. He is so sure. His tongue is deft and strong and slides expertly along her teeth. Oh, she could like this guy very much. She pulls away and snorts. 'That guy's face!'

He mimes boggling shock. '"Hey! My car! A girl's bottom on my car!"'

'My bum made such a dint.'

He squeezes it appreciatively. 'Such a big bum.'

Wide eyes. 'It is not.'

'*Un bel culo. Culo basso.* Low arse.'

'It is *not*!'

His eyes manage to laugh even as his face is serious. 'What a nice arse. What a lovely arse. I want to take a bite out of it.'

'It is *not big*.'

'Just perfect.' He is so happy. As they enter the long grassy oval of Circus Maximus he looks around. There are only a few figures at the far end, way too distant and shadowed to see anything, but he makes an exaggerated show of being furtive, then leads her quickly across the road to a ramp with a parapet that leads up to an ancient garage. Their lower halves are hidden now but they're in view of the passing traffic. He wraps himself around her, plunges against her hips. There is the pressure of a belly on her; he's not thin. Along the road the cars make a bucketing sound on the cobbles. His hand pulls at her jeans; she unzips them and pushes them down a little. Three fingers slick up and down her cleft; one thickly penetrates her; she quivers around it. His naked cock is very, very hard against her hip. He jigs down a fraction, to get access; the first time, he misses the mark, then he's in.

Oh my god, she thinks. I'm fucking up against a wall in the Circus Maximus. I'm fucking this guy in public. No condom, she thinks, too late. Around her a summer wind tousles the trees and her hair; she feels as careless. Against her bare buttocks the old wall scrapes and flakes with every thrust.

They clutch and pant. He is gasping into her ear, frantic and helpless, his hands firm on her hips. Oh, that's good. Oh, that's good. She loves the sound of his seizing, that she can do this to someone; he's crooning desperately now; he chokes; she shoves him away roughly and holds his cock in her hand as he finishes. The fluid drips onto the gravel below like some ancient sacrifice. She holds him and holds him until they're quiet; then they look at each other and beam.

'My, my,' she says in English. 'Aren't we the little firecracker?'

'You are beautiful,' he breathes. He grimaces as he puts his penis away, kisses her on the lips. 'What a beautiful girl. Your soul is beautiful.'

She's caught between amusement and disappointment. Well, he should think she's beautiful, after she's just let him fuck her on a first date without a condom; still, how often has she heard that airy word? But he says it so earnestly, so wide-eyed and wondering.

He adds, 'It doesn't matter about the outside.' He's not teasing. How marvellous, not to be bullshitted about being beautiful when she is not.

She winks at him; yanks up her pants; pats the wall she's been leaning on. 'Thank you, wall.'

'Thank you, wall,' he echoes.

At the bottom of the ramp she straightens her shoulders. 'Well. That was lovely.' She starts giggling again. 'That was very nice. Thank you for the pizza,' she tries to say gravely. 'Thank you for dinner.'

'Tomorrow?'

She has a feeling that, if she says yes, she'll spend a great deal more time looking at him like this, awaiting something delightful. It's good to make him wait, but, 'Bloody hell, give me your number.' She writes it in her notebook. Looks up at him, and gives him a quick, grateful kiss on each cheek and a final one on his lips. He smells fucking wonderful. 'So. I'll call you.'

He stands there and calls, 'Bye Katie. You're beautiful. Beautiful bottom! Big bum girl!' She hears his voice calling even as she walks away.

✦

The next day he meets her in the sunshine at the train station; his high forehead is shiny with sweat. He looks different this afternoon: the nice suit is gone, he is in old work pants and runners, a baggy T-shirt emblazoned in violent yellow, and a baseball cap ripped on one side. He may be the worst-dressed Italian she has ever seen. Before she finds him in the crowd she feels his eyes on her: those strange green eyes humid with feeling. He doesn't smile as she greets him, but fixes her with a look that suggests he is seconds away from ravishing her. Then he squeezes her arse so firmly she can feel one finger reaching around beneath to press inside. Her eyes widen as she lurches off-balance. He catches her and relents and there it is, that faun-like grin. His cheek is moist and hot when she kisses it.

He tells her he's taken the afternoon off work.

'Off work? Can you do that?'

His housemates are all at the yard, he explains. They share a small place—she thinks he says they share a bed, but that can't be right—and it will be empty until dinnertime. He raises his eyebrow, waggles it and makes a kissy mouth, jerking his head back.

'Carm won, babby,' he says. She cups his head in one hand. 'Come on, baby,' she repeats in his accent. They get a train. On the way he holds her tight, amid the standing passengers; they kiss and she catches the disapproving glare of a matron; from the corner of her eye she glares back and kisses him harder.

He lives a long way out. A long, long way. This is hardly Rome as she knows it: the modern apartment blocks, like her own, replicate the old ones but these are monotonous, sunblasted, tacky-looking. It is ridiculously hot for February. 'How much further?' she pants, desperate for a drink. He turns, catches her hand. 'Not far.'

The apartment is smaller than hers: two bedrooms, a lounge room that smells of sweaty feet. Men live here. It seems she heard right: there are seven men living here and only five beds. Not much in the way of clothing or personal belongings: they have travelled light, bringing only work gear and something fancy for a Saturday night. The shutters are all down and the apartment is gloomy with shadows but cool. Gabriele pours water from a bottle into a glass; she drinks gratefully. He watches. Then they go into the bedroom with only two beds. They sit on a double bed, its sheets neatly tucked. 'Is this your one?'

He shakes his head. He pulls her onto his lap. 'Beautiful Katie.' He examines her face, his hand stroking her hair. He looks at her throat, her collar bones, runs his palms down the length of her arms. She grows self-conscious. There is something frighteningly tender about this looking. As if he is preparing for something important, not simply a fuck, not just the mashing of bodies together.

He arrives at the scars on the crooks of her arm. She holds her breath as he rubs each one with the tip of a finger.

'*Non sono perfetta*,' she says. She meant it to come out strong; but it is a whisper. She bows her head. He touches them so delicately. 'I'm not perfect, Gabriele.'

'No one is perfect,' he murmurs, and pulls her so that as he falls back on the bed she comes easily to rest upon him.

+

He's not exactly fat, but upholstered with that gleaming olive-oil skin that Nanni had, the suggestion of plump recently escaped from in young manhood, to come again in middle age. He has a belly round and solid, a firm line of hair down his chest, and the most beautiful shoulders she's ever seen. Sitting astride him she holds them in her hands, strong balls of muscle and bone. He looks up at her, curious. She grits her teeth and clenches them harder. 'Oh,' she says in ecstasy, 'I could just fucking *break you*.'

The look he gives dares her to.

Sex with Gabriele is like his conversation: a mixture of the intently serious and the teasing. But he is assured in bed; his confidence surprises her. He pulls her up, presses her down; he yanks her legs around his waist, her arms about his neck, rises to his feet, and swings her like a pendulum in and away from him; she stares into his face. He plays her supple body, she is enthralled. But there is no suggestion of bullying. He kisses her often, sweetly, fiercely; their bodies are slick with sweat and between his hands she feels secure.

He comes lying on top of her, climbing her body into the bed. Before his breath has calmed she feels him grow heavy—heavier—his head drops against her neck; he is asleep. She lies there, still panting (but quietly, not to wake him), with her hand stuck with sweat to his ribs, feeling this sturdy furniture-maker loosen above her like a child.

He wakes after a few minutes and gazes at her groggily. 'Beautiful, beautiful,' he murmurs, and rolls off her.

They shower—he conscientiously shows her a clean towel, the soap, the taps. She lets him, trying not to laugh. Modestly, he leaves her alone to wash. When she gets out of the water he shows her how to put oil on her wet skin and pats her dry with the towel, flops a fold of it over her eyes. He pokes her in the middle and bites her ear.

They are in the kitchen, drinking small cups of coffee, when his workmates return. She is introduced to various dark-haired, tired-looking men in dirty clothes. They are perplexed to find a girl in their kitchen but greet her politely. There isn't room for them all. When she goes to the bathroom again she sees that her chin is rubbed pink and raw from Gabriele's stubble; what a picture she must have made to his friends. Gabriele knocks and enters, to make sure she has found the toilet paper. Tutting, he finds some ointment in the cupboard, smoothes it on her chin as tenderly as a grandmother.

He takes her back to the station, and they sit on the train sleepily, his baseball cap foolish on her head. She feels like a teenager sitting next to her first boyfriend. She leans against Gabriele's shoulder, and he puts his arm around her.

They part at the gate to her apartment; he has the long journey home again now. Before he walks away he kisses her so fiercely she staggers.

✦

After all this, to be picked up in the street by a ridiculous Italian. Really, she thinks crossly but smiling, you'd think I'd never learned anything. Still, here she is, with Gabriele's joyful voice on the phone, his call from below the balcony when he has finished work and crossed all of Rome to collect her, the way he kisses her in greeting half-playful, half-ravenous: all this makes her sprawl on the couch with anticipation as the days warm and Rome opens. She loves the anticipation of the night's ramble and their giggling search for somewhere to make love (for she is reluctant to bring him home to Tom's flat); they fuck in Circus Maximus, under trees, in silent lanes, against ancient walls; she presses her face into Gabriele's throat as they walk home. He is exactly the same height as her. Arm-in-arm strolling doesn't quite work but they hold hands always, instead. She learns that she need only turn her face a little as they walk together, for him swiftly to kiss her lips and reel away, looking as drunk with astonishment as she feels.

Tom says nothing, only rolls his eyes when she hastens back from the balcony and grabs her bag to rush downstairs. 'Try not to get arrested,' he calls.

They are lovers. They drink wine in piazzas, they molest each other in parks. Often, excited, he speaks too rapidly for her to follow; she watches his mouth, the confidence of it pronouncing what suddenly seem outlandish syllables—he has a strong Napoletano accent that makes the language mischievous, lascivious, where he is saying only, 'My father grows his own tomatoes.' He talks dialect with her; he teaches her obscenities she can never fix in her memory, so sibilant are the words in her mouth. He will sit and gravely take her hands in his and spill a torrent of endearments: You are my immense treasure, my beautiful star, heart of my heart, my soul of love…Is he taking the piss? No. There are tears in his eyes. Overwhelmed by the rapid language and the emotion, she listens to his soul of love.

Gabriele, I know you best through your eyes.

Able to communicate only in his language, she improves quickly, learning it *dalla bocca*, from the mouth of her lover. There is no vocabulary for nervousness in her Italian, no words that she has learned yet for 'doubt', 'angst', 'disturbed young woman'. The language in her mouth is crude, direct, literal; the accent is terrible, she cannot roll her 'r's, the flamboyance of Italian is beyond her. She hasn't mastered idioms; she is content to find the basic words. It seems that without the words for doubt, there are no doubts.

She learns from him to say, '*Hai capito?*' Did you understand? It is said in the past tense, it seems, not the present she had previously used. He says it often: '*Hai capito*, Katie? *Hai capito?*' He wants her to understand, to pay attention, to follow him.

There are three ways to say 'I love you', he tells her. '*Ti voglio bene*' is what you say to a friend. It charms her: 'I want you well.' But to a lover you say '*ti amo*' or, even more romantically, '*ti adoro*.'

'*Ti adoro*, Katie,' he says looking into her eyes very still and close. '*Ti adoro per sempre*.'

'*Ti adoro*, Gabriele,' she breathes back.

He shows her a photo of him, aged twenty, in his National Service army uniform; on his laughing young head is a cap, a paper butterfly pinned to it. 'Why the butterfly?' she asks.

'*Per bellezza*,' he says. 'For beauty.'

The bonnet of the wretched car will cost four hundred euro to fix. Awed, she puts it in Australian dollars. Six hundred bucks. She offers to help pay, horrified by the waste of her dwindling savings but obligated by love—and somewhere along the line it has stopped being his fault, but theirs together, for he was right to seduce her. He adamantly refuses. Even when she discovers he has spent his last money (the coins he carefully thumbs from his wallet) on a tray of claggy cakes for her, he won't let her help him pay.

His job is tough, tiring and precarious. It's unusual for a boy from Napoli to travel for work, on spec; he misses home; she sheepishly compares his travails with her own fortune in saving money and living overseas unemployed, doing as she likes. He starts at eight o'clock, stands labouring hard until six, showers, shaves and comes an hour on the train to find her. He falls asleep over their cheap meals, falls asleep right in front of her eyes, still sitting; she watches him as if he might dissolve to dust. He opens his eyes, sees her there, and leans his heavy head against her shoulder.

In bed, 'Don't you want to make love?' she whispers.

'This is enough. Come closer to me. Close to me. Sleep.'

He is her boy, her non-book-reading, hard-working, callous-handed, honey-kissing, cake-buying carpenter boy from Naples.

'You are my precious, my sweet Katie,' he says. He borrows her small dictionary; looks up eagerly from the page. He says in English, 'You my sweat Katie. My sweat.'

'I am your sweat?'

'You my sweat,' he repeats, earnest, loving. She gasps with laughter.

'Sweet. Sweet, Gabriele!'

But he never mocks her clumsy Italian; never minds when she, missing a crucial vowel, says, 'You or me or she? Who? Who are you talking about?' He will always tell her everything twice, three times, as many as it takes for her to understand that she is his precious, his *immenso amore*, his sweet girl. He buys her a gelato the next time he has money and insists on cream being stuffed into the cone, cream inside and cream on the top. He could afford only the one. She eats it lovingly: she is getting fat and she doesn't care. Everything is filling out. Her hair is growing longer now.

✦

There comes a moment when she dares assume Tom will understand, and she sneaks Gabriele in through the front door late one night and quickly into her room; what difference will it make if he arrives after Tom is asleep and leaves early in the morning? They awake the next day, after the heaven of sleeping plaited together in her narrow single bed, and he kisses her good morning, scours her stale mouth with his tongue, grins and goes to make coffee in Tom's kitchen. He brings it to her: very milky coffee, 'for the bowels,' he tells her. He dresses quickly, unwashed, without drinking a coffee himself, for he has to cross Rome to get to work in time. She sits up, holds her arms out. 'Stay,' she entreats, 'stay,' and presses her breasts up into his leaning embrace. He kisses her swiftly, pats her naked arse—'Look after that,' he instructs— and is gone.

Tom says nothing, except to ask that Gabriele makes sure he's out of the bathroom before Tom needs it, 'Because an old man needs to piss when he needs to piss.'

There comes a time when she looks at Gabriele, fussing over the service in a cheap and crappy *tavola calda*, getting cross, and can see him as a man in his fifties, the father he has shown her photos of, ravine-jawed, trim, full of rectitude, lover of vine tomatoes, reader of the sports pages. He admires his father very much. She finds herself examining the son. Yes, he'll keep losing his hair. But he has good, supple, olive skin. He's not tall, but he's funny. Is he bright? She looks at his eyes, shining with triumph and humour as they walk away from the restaurant, and she thinks: he is as bright as a star.

There comes a time when she clasps his hips as she slides down the bed and looks up at him and suddenly finds the words 'marry me' in her throat. Surprised, she swallows them down; opens her mouth, takes him in it instead.

There comes a time when she looks at his mouth, which can be so agile and so merry, or so full and luscious with feeling, or so messy as he gapes with his crooked tooth and his boy's smile over a mouthful of salad, and marvels that she has found herself this sweet holy fool who seems to have so little in the world, but gives her everything.

He has the ability to make her dissolve with desire, just from letting his face go still and gazing at her.

There comes a time, in the weeks that pass, when she ceases to question this great joy of finding a man simple, brave and true, who isn't fucked up inside, who doesn't play games, who holds her carefully in the warm room so she won't fall from the bed but refuses to leave the window open for fresh air, who shares nothing of her world or her interests, who is the most beautiful creature to her and makes her a part of this country: no longer an interloper, but a lover. She watches him as he sleeps, to make sure his dream isn't disturbed.

Here, far from her own home, there is so little of her. None of her books, her belongings, her music. None of her friends, to reflect her to him. It is just herself, her body and her thoughts. Just her, just her that he loves.

And her past. He knows about the scars, he hasn't asked more. It is the great proof of his faith in her.

She hesitates, she has hesitated for weeks. But he is a man of Naples, he knows the underside of the world, he won't be scared. She owes it to him, there can be no secrets between them. She imagines his pitying look, his solid arms embracing her, the more understanding for the fact that she has trusted him.

And she says it, the two of them sitting on a bench outside an ancient church. 'Gabriele, I have to tell you something. I was a—' She still has to use the word, oh this second before she says it, this hard moment, '—a *puttana*.' She makes herself look at him. Each time she has told this, a little more skin has been shed.

He narrows his eyes, but they are soft, he sits and listens.

She explains a little—the drug habit, how much money she needed, how it became more than just cash, it saved her in a way, the emotion of it, how lonely she was then, how—

'*Va bene*,' he says. '*Ho capito. Ho capito*, Katie,' and he reaches forward, pulls her head towards his chest, wraps her up. She rests. His chest is broad and deep, his carpenter's muscles, his slow breathing. '*Basta*. You don't have to explain. I know you, you are a beautiful girl, you are my *tesoro*.'

'You don't mind?' she says into his chest.

'No. I don't mind. I love you, you are my *immenso amore*.' He raises her, kisses her lips, then her brow. '*Ti amo*, Katie.' The feeling in his eyes is almost unbearable. '*Ti adoro per sempre.*'

'Forever, forever,' she whispers. There are tears on her lashes before he kisses them away.

✦

Tom sits her at the table one night before Gabriele arrives and, beer in hand, fixes her with a look. 'Are you going to marry him?'

'What?'

'Could you marry him? Is he the one?'

'Jesus. I don't think about it like that. We're just going out. We've only been together for a couple of months.'

'But do you love him?'

She thinks: Well, you've met him. You've seen him. How could I not be in love with him? Gabriele eating with gusto, Gabriele bright with mischief as he tells a joke in Italian that Tom can't possibly follow, Gabriele solicitously—almost to the point of mania—worrying about the kind of salt they have in their kitchen, not iodised, very bad, he tuts, very, very bad. She knows Gabriele drives Tom mad but he must love him too, no one could not.

'I love him. I love him so much. He loves me back.' It's true. She can say it without fear.

'Well then.'

'But marry...' She shakes her head. 'I dunno. I don't really imagine getting married to anyone. I'm not that type.'

'It might do you good. Some sense of responsibility. Don't laugh. You need it. You could have kids.'

'Kids,' she scoffs. How did he know that she's been dreaming, wondering what a baby with Gabriele would look like, how it would have his glossy skin, his merry eyes, those sweet crooked teeth? That Gabriele had already joked about it, half-

184

seriously; she isn't taking the pill or using condoms, she is daring her body to make a baby. 'One thing at a time.'

'But do you have anything in common? Does he read?'

'Nope.'

'Does he like the same things as you? Does he even know what you like? I don't know what you like and I've been suffering living with you for bloody years now.'

'Months, dear. Months, not years.'

'Feels like centuries. But are you compatible? It's no good if you're not. It's just a holiday romance. Face it. It's just a fling. Something out of your bloody books.'

Now she frowns. 'It's not. It's much more than that. Just because we're from different countries...Rome's full of couples where someone came here and fell in love with an Italian and stayed. It happens all the time. It's entirely possible.'

'But is that what *you're* doing? Are you going to stay, get a job, and marry him and live together? Take him to Australia in your luggage? You have to look ahead, girlie. You have to get your head out of your fanny and *think*.'

But that feels like hard work. She's thought too much. She's worked too hard. She wants only to float on this great joy, which she deserves—which she *deserves*, she whispers to herself later—and be happy when she looks into her *amore*'s eyes and he looks back and they are both so *allegri*, so *felici*, so *innamorati*, so in love.

✦

She is in a daydream of moving to Italy permanently ('Where's Kate these days?' 'Oh, she married an Italian. She lives in Naples in an old palazzo with their seventeen children. Blissfully happy.') when the phone rings. She springs to it—has he finished work early?

'*Ciao principessa.*'

'Massimo!'

'*Sì*! It's Massimo. Massimo, your Jame Bond.'

My god, has it been so long? 'Hey bravo, how are you?'

'Very good, *bene, benissimo. Senti*, next week is my *compleanno*, my, how you say, birthday. I have a party. Another party. I want that you come.'

'Oh.' She thinks. Mmm. Gabriele…'In Napoli?'

'Yes, of course. *Ho riservato un bar*, everyone come, Nanni, Allegra, you know Allegra…'

'You two are still together?' She is glad.

'Yes, she is patient with me. You come, Karty, I dance with you, we do sexy dance…'

'I don't dance.' She is giggling; how is it, even after she has understood him so well, Massimo still makes her jolly? She can see him on the other end of the phone, cheerfully enticing her. 'Okay. When is it?'

He gives her the details. She asks after Nanni ('Ah, he is sad, no sex since you left.' 'I don't believe it for a minute.') and they hang up. She goes to the balcony to smoke and think. Gabriele won't like it. She hasn't told him about Massimo. Only that she has friends in Naples. She'll work something out. Why shouldn't she go to her friend's party? It is only a party.

In fact Gabriele is pleased by the news that she's going down to see a friend, because he has planned to visit his parents there the same weekend. He is often homesick; it's hard for a southern boy to be far from his mama. He hesitates, however: 'I am sorry, Katie, I cannot take you to meet them.' A story about how he was once engaged. The girl broke his parents' heart: they'd taken her to their bosom and she'd broken it off. He looks upset. 'Maybe one day.' She assures him it's okay; there is just a twinge in her, again to be the hidden woman. Crouching

186

beneath the dashboard of Jack's car. The luggage cupboard at Hotel Fiamma. 'It's fine, I'll stay in a hotel and we can meet up when you're free.'

Not Hotel Fiamma, obviously. Even she's not so crass. Nor Massimo's apartment, not if she's going to fuck Gabriele in his home city. She's excited at the prospect of seeing it through his eyes. As she gets the familiar train down there on the Friday afternoon the memories come back. All good memories, now. Only good memories. She's delighted to be returning. A woman with a boyfriend, a romantic weekend.

She finds the hotel she's booked, a small one in a palazzo near the church of the Gesù. A small boy greets her at the door, wordlessly escorts her to a salon off the hall. Her footsteps are loud on the cold tiled floor. A shadowed figure sits in an armchair against the drawn curtains, terrible as an oracle.

'*Buona sera, signora.*'

A hairy chin is lifted in assent; a taloned hand gestures to the boy.

'*Numero tre,*' he whispers, and puts a key in her hand.

The room is not spooky, however, just tacky in the same vein as the Fiamma. Same fluorescent strip lights, same kind of 1970s bedspread. She can't help but feel cheered. Hilariously, she thinks it's a good room for a suicide. She rings Gabriele at work. 'I'm already here. What time are you getting to your parents'? Are you sure you don't want to come?' She has asked Massimo if she might bring a guest; she didn't say what kind, but she was surprised when he said it was perhaps better if she didn't. Then he relented. She considers Massimo a friend now. So why shouldn't she bring her own lover? She wants Massimo to see her new triumph. She thinks they might like each other.

But Gabriele says no, he won't come, better that he doesn't.

He admonishes her at length to watch out, take care, '*stare attenta*'. She sighs.

That night she is picked up from the piazza by a friend of Massimo's, a middle-aged man with a wild shag of hair called Angelo. He talks and smokes non-stop on their drive to the bar—she loses track of where it is, somewhere on the expensive heights of Posillipo. Inside, Massimo comes forth with his arms outstretched. 'My *principessa*. Hello, honey. Here is a drink. Honey, honey,' he says, lowering his voice and whispering into her ear. 'I miss you so much. My *cazzo* misses you.'

She kisses his cheek, happy. 'I bet your *cazzo* has been busy.'

They look over at Allegra, exquisite in a white silk dress, her wide kind smile as she has her glass filled by an attentive Franco with the goatee and glasses.

'Never enough. But listen,' he says louder, 'Where is your friend?'

'He couldn't come. Parents,' she grimaces. Massimo nods, uninterested.

'*Allora*. Have a drink, have fun. All good friends here.'

No sign of Guido, thank god. She spies Nanni, lugubrious but smiling. He greets her sweetly, finds her a place to sit.

'How's...' She indicates Massimo.

He shakes his head. 'I don't know. Still *pazzo*. For example, he have two birthdays, one for family, this one with Allegra. He make big risks,' and he shrugs.

'And you, Nanni?'

'I am okay. *Bene*. I stay home with my wife, I dream of girls, I am a good guy.' He looks mournful. But then he kisses her on the cheek. 'I am lucky. I have good memories.'

It's a cheerful party. Allegra and she catch each other's smiles; various people ask where her boyfriend is and sympathise that he couldn't come, even criticise him for letting such a lovely girl out on her own; her Italian survives the noise; she escapes having to dance by hiding with Nanni, who only swings her hand in time to the music. She feels her phone buzz in her pocket and goes outside to answer it. The night is fresh and from the parapet of this bar there is a view of the black sea.

'Yes, my *dolce amore*? Are you here in Napoli?'

He sends a smacky kiss noise down the phone. '*Buona sera*,' he says in his sing-song way, so that 'sera' sounds like 'seera'. He sounds tired. 'How was the party?'

'I'm still here.'

'Still there?' He sounds shocked. 'It is midnight.'

'It's a good party.' He's such a grandmother sometimes. 'I'm having a great time. Are you sure you don't want to come?'

Silence. Then, 'I see you tomorrow. Go home soon, Katie, and watch out.' *Stare attenta.*

A little aggrieved, she returns to the party. It doesn't last much longer; Massimo arranges a lift with Angelo and others. She kisses him goodbye with a particular fervour, meaning *Look after yourself, you goose.* 'Talk soon,' he promises. Genial cries of farewell, shrugging on of elegant jackets; the group spills out and disperses. She is dropped back at the vast medieval portal of her hotel, blunders under the bedcovers and falls asleep.

The next morning, in brilliant sunshine, she meets Gabriele in the piazza. He's looking holidayish in an open-necked shirt and gigantic sunglasses: the very image of an Italian boyfriend. She eyes his daffodil-yellow trousers with some amazement, but throws her arm over his shoulders. He hands her a take-away espresso and a cornetto pastry. Doesn't he realise she's had breakfast at the hotel? Perhaps he's never stayed in a hotel.

When she's finished eating he leans in and licks the sugar dust from the corner of her mouth.

'Oh, my *amore*,' she says.

'Oh, my *tesoro*,' he says kissing her cheek, and they stroll off. There is a puppet show in one corner of the piazza, and a big crowd. They stop to watch, but the act is all in dialect.

'What are they saying?'

He shrugs. 'It's traditional.'

She watches the costumes, the elaborate puppets, the shouted lines that have the audience screaming.

'They've been doing it for hundreds of years,' he says, bored, and leads her away. 'Come on, baby.'

It is a Naples day indeed. He shows her where he grew up, in Spaccanapoli, the true rotting core of the city, the dense labyrinth of streets, the buildings even more scrofulous here and no room for sunlight. He is proud of the place: 'I am *vero napoletano*,' he says. She imagines him at six years old, skinny in a white singlet, running through shadows. They leave quickly. Gabriele already warned her, as if she'd never been to Naples before, to watch her belongings, keep hold of her purse; he has an anxious, alert air. Even a *vero napoletano* might get robbed. She reminds him that she has walked around here on her own, and never had any trouble.

He has borrowed his father's car and is relieved to see it still safely parked. They drive out to the west, into the Campi Flegrei area, stopping to buy ham rolls and drinks. Along a freeway, smaller roads, past leafy glades; they pull up in a wooded area with a parapet and an entrance sign. 'Cuma,' he says. 'Very nice place.'

It's like walking into a dream. There are no other visitors. Saplings and old trees grow thick and still here. A dank passage formed from great stones: the Sibyl's grotto. They walk in the cool mossy corridor, silenced, as doves fluster from their nooks and the echoes sound like catastrophe. She ducks as a bird darts past her head. The end of the corridor is empty, but it has an eerie atmosphere. They fingertip the rough stones.

The path leads on, past ruins of temples and great oak trees. Sunshine soaks through the leaves; it is cool in the shade, in the vents where the sea breeze comes through; they are high above the sea now. They walk holding hands, unspeaking. Light is like blessing.

He draws her off the path and into a glade of grass, pulls her to sit. They eat their food. 'It's wonderful, Gabriele,' she says.

They lie down in the grass, in the green shadows, and fall asleep.

She wakes with his mouth on her hair, nuzzling. Her eyes are closed, her limbs heavy as if soaked in water. Drowsy, she stirs, his lips are on hers, she opens her mouth and his tongue is as delicious as wine. He is moving slowly, smoothly; she is limp, giving, and when he pushes her skirt high she lets her thighs fall luxuriously open, slow as breathing.

And he is kissing her. And his fingers are inside her moving delicate as whispers, and they send spangles of joy through her, something that may become unbearable, which becomes so sharp that she gasps into his open mouth, she bites his lip as the spangles become spikes, and the sour-sweet piercing is more than she can bear. Through the great heaviness of her body a thrust of urgency makes her breath stop, stop, stop; she fills her skin and she is coming, coming as instantly, as sweetly as being forgiven.

✛

On the train back to Rome she is telling him cheerfully— finally—about her friends in Naples. Massimo's party, the complications with Allegra, how she also knew Guido, the way Nanni makes her laugh…Gabriele watches her, his eyes narrowed.

'They are not friends.'

'Of course they are.' Oh, she hoped he wouldn't feel like this, wouldn't blame her for having partners before him; she's nearly thirty, for god's sake. She wants him to know how grateful she is for the times she had in Naples, in his own town, how they prepared her for him. She refuses to let this be difficult, an obstacle. 'Of course they are. They were my lovers, but they're also friends. We talked, we made jokes. They're nice guys. They looked after me. Massimo—'

'But not friends.' His face is dark, mulish. It infuriates her; this is his father coming out. And jealousy. How dull: she expected better of him. 'You're innocent. They took advantage of you.'

She flares. 'How can *you* know? I'm not so innocent. It was a game, a good game. I know how to play it.' Doesn't she? If she knows anything. 'I'm not *innocent*,' she says again.

'No, you have done things, you're not innocent, you're right. But that's why it's bad. How can you have done what you did, before, and not know any better now?'

He is facing her. He raises his hand and pushes her shoulder—once, twice. He shoves her hard. 'No. They did not respect you. You don't respect yourself. Don't you realise?'

Grinning in shock and fury, she can't speak. How can she explain? Being light is not a crime. Loving more than one man is not a diminishing.

She has been through all this, over and over. Oh *god*. She stares at him, incandescent. If only she didn't have to put it in Italian, if she could explain—how she can't believe she was wrong—she was right, she was right, how else might she have ended up here, so wise to her blessings? Massimo's diabolical laugh, Nanni's jokes, her body cherished and singing—all the things she's achieved. How can he expect her to repent? And this jibe about the prostitution—how dare he use that against her? When she trusted him? It is monstrous. It is obscene.

She doesn't respect herself?

She opens her mouth to speak; but abruptly doesn't know what she might say.

Their knees are entwined as they sit opposite each other on the tacky plastic seats on the local train from Termini to her flat. She tries to keep her legs away from his; he presses his closer. She is rigid. Wriggling, he captures her legs in his; she knows if she looked up he would be giving her a teasing smile, to relinquish the tension. She won't look up from her hands that are clenched in her lap.

*Puttana.*

Is she, is she, is she?

She has only tried to make herself happy.

Other people happy.

Perhaps she was wrong.

What does she know of the rules? If you are used, but you consent, is it still wrong? Where is the space for simplicity, for something easy and free? A rhyme that won't come right, that stumbles on her tongue.

Does it matter?

As they are walking home in silence he hesitates, and pulls a white flower from a vine that has climbed a wall. He holds it in his fingers like a burning match. She waits, hopeless, dumb with defeat.

He walks towards her. Holds out the flower. She won't take it.

'*Ecco.* A white flower for you, who loves white flowers. You are my flower, Katie.'

She takes it then, holds it in loose fingers. Her voice is dull. 'I'm not a flower, Gabriele. Maybe I'm just a stupid girl.'

He says nothing, only looks at her in pity.

Later, clammy in the hot airless room, she lies awake with her mouth against Gabriele's shoulder. Her flesh softens with misery.

And comfort? Is that not allowed?

The words *felicità, tenerezza, dolcezza* form on her lips, whisper against Gabriele's skin. *Happiness. Tenderness. Sweetness.*

Gabriele stirs and sighs and grasps her more tightly. His hand is moist with sleep and heavy on hers; it loosens, but does not fall away. Outside she hears the trees, and a motorbike thudding past. She stays awake for a long time, staring at the window in the dark, whispering, her heart fast and hot, thinking of trajectories.

part six

# DONATELLA

*It is in giving yourself that you possess yourself.*
**LOU ANDREAS-SALOMÉ**

It is over a year later. She sits on a train rattling through northern Italy, a land champagne-coloured with light. It is the hottest summer in memory. It seems the heat has seeped through the sealed train windows; her very heart is boiling with nervousness.

On her phone, Byron's signet ring inscription: *Elle vous suit partout*. She follows you everywhere.

She is heading north to see her love, to whom she has been so faithful.

There came a moment, the year before, when she realised she was soon going to run out of money. She contemplated staying in Italy and getting a job—but what job? With no references and her poor Italian? She has been living in a paradise, in Tom's flat; Tom is leaving Rome; Gabriele still shares a bed with a housemate. There is no way they can do this now. She has been in Europe nearly a year. Rome is greasy with sunshine and the crowds are congealing in the piazzas. She and Gabriele have been together for three months; the city has swollen with warmth around them, they are bound now, their hands find each other even in sleep. But she must go home and get a job to make money, in order to return.

*Marry me* pressed up in her throat, unsaid.

The tears on their cheeks at the airport; she nearly missed the plane.

How stale and cold her room in Melbourne was; she rushed to check her email every day, deciphering the floods of loving declarations, injunctions to look after herself, reports of what he'd eaten for lunch, the refrain: you are my sweet treasure, my soul, flower of my heart. She conjured him every day, until she almost mumbled the flavour out of her memories. For over a year. She wore a talisman of him around her throat. He was warm water around her loneliness.

'Marry me,' he said on the phone one night.

'Yes,' she said, 'yes. Yes.'

It was so enormous, they didn't mention it again.

On the phone, in their rushed calls in his lunchtime, her midnight, it is hard to follow his words without the gestures, his laughing eyes, his hand squeezing hers for emphasis. She simply listens to his voice, its dear huskiness. He tells her over and over to look after herself. She understands that part. *I love you, I miss you,* they murmur, until the words are made stupid. She has waited up until one a.m., to catch him in his lunch break. The line is bad. They do this every week, once a week only, for twenty minutes. Sometimes she can't get through at all.

'*Non ho capito,*' she says, '*dispiace,* Gabriele, *non ho capito.*'

He repeats. Still: no, she doesn't quite catch the words.

Something about lunch. Something about love? His voice fading, the sounds of the workyard behind him, her ear pressed so hard against the phone in the warm night, he says it's so cold there. 'I wish I could be there,' she says, 'I wish I could warm you, my *amore,* my *tesoro.*

'No. *Non ho capito. Ti amo,* Gabriele, *ti amo.*

'Yes. Oh, I miss Roma, so much. *Sì. Sì. Roma mi manca, molto.* I miss you. *Mi manchi tu.*

'Okay, *va bene*. *Ciao, tesoro, ciao, ciao, ciao…*'

A noise in the hall as she hangs up. Her mother, squinting in a nightgown. 'Sorry, Mum.'

'Did you get hold of him?'

'Yes. He's okay. He sends his love to you. He says make sure I eat enough.'

Her mother smiles. 'He's so gorgeous. Tell him we want him to visit here. Tell him we have pasta here, too.'

She throws the used phone card in the bin. 'I don't think he believes Australia really exists. You just tumble over the end of the world and that's it.'

Six months later she borrows money, packs a bag, seals a box of her essential belongings to be sent on later, maybe. Outside Rome airport she sheds her last winter clothes and gasps in the dry hot air. A night in a hotel, barely pausing, onto a train. It stirs out of Termini gathering pace, she peers out towards the city she has missed so fiercely; she will be back, surely, but Gabriele doesn't live here anymore. Her orientation has changed.

He has moved north for work, to a small town near Padua. Again, a house full of blokes. He has grown dispirited in his emails, it sounds like a dull place. She sent sympathy: letters, presents, compilation CDs. Her endless devotion. Devoted enough to say that he may fuck someone else, only use a condom, don't fall in love, and tell her. She is proud of herself for this worldliness; Italian men, she tells her friends, need sex, I don't mind, I know he loves me. With mock exasperation she says, He says he doesn't want anyone else, anyway.

But on the phone he is always rushed; he works twelve hours. No time for sex, not even emails. Humiliation grates in his voice. He complains there is nothing to do; he has started jogging. He's exhausted, their calls so hurried he makes a mistake, says '*ti voglio bene*'; she lets it pass, compassionate. He is so poor, he jokes, he eats nothing but beans, like a peasant. She brings Australian biscuits, chocolate in her bag, she brings herself to nourish him now.

The train takes seven hours. She is hardly able to believe she is on it.

'*Are you still coming?*'

'*Should I?*'

+

The early evening air is dry and stinking hot. She gets off the train in a muddle of passengers, tugs her bag onto the platform, gazes around. She does not want him to find her looking lost. She has gone three steps before something catches her collar; she spins; his mouth is on her before she can breathe. She buries her face in his throat. Around them people eddy, bang into each other; he holds her tight and she sucks in his scent.

'*Tesoro.*'

'*Tesoro.*'

But she almost doesn't recognise him when she raises her face. He is lean, his hair shorn, his face sharp with definition. Is he taller? There is no comfortable belly pressing against hers; he is pared down, taut and straight where before he was all curves. He takes her bag and leads her to the car; he is smiling at her; for once she's the one doing all the talking. His eyes seem a different colour—more hazel—but make the same sweet shapes. How much thinner he is! On the drive to his place they hold hands, his smile is as sweet and catlike as ever, but he has to remove his hand often to change gear. The landscape they pass through is flat, peaceful, desiccated to yellow, interrupted with freeways and factory sheds and banks of reeds by the kerb.

His house is empty; the others are away for a few days. He

lives in a house with a messy yard, on the outskirts of a small town. It's like country Australia. Dogs bark in the distance. He carries her bag up the stairs. Just like the first time he took her to his house in Rome, all the shutters are drawn. Their rush of talk ceases.

In the gloomy kitchen he shreds lettuce and puts coffee on and then, abruptly, passing her, sinks his mouth into hers, making her totter. He kisses her hand and looks up, bright and intent. 'You're here, finally here,' he says. He lifts her onto the kitchen bench. Presses closer.

For the first time she needn't stifle her noises as they grapple. It is fucking, desperate and gasping, fingers digging into shoulders, lips bitten, skin grown slick. She leaves a sweat print on the bench. It has been so long since she was penetrated; her body hasn't yet remembered how to do this. He comes as if crying.

The cafetiére boils.

They lie on a small divan in the kitchen as night falls, the lettuce going yellow, the coffee pot full. He wraps her from behind. Though the evening is stifling she pulls his arm more tightly around her; he strokes her breast, then falters to stillness. He breathes in once, deeply, then out. After a few minutes she disengages, stands and turns to look at him. A newly thinned angel, arm loose across his breathing chest, jointed and sheened like a wing bone. He looks vulnerable and beautiful. She kisses his damp skin all over, shyly, with slow lips, as the weatherman on the television says it is thirty-nine degrees.

✦

'You're hot,' she says foolishly. It is three in the afternoon of the next day. The big white bed in his room. Fleshly scents rise from their bodies. Light creams fuzzily along the line of him.

The heat is a dream, soporific. They lie there smiling at each other, and breathe shallowly like animals.

They take the day slowly, much of it in bed touching, whispering. He is off work for the month and time is like syrup. They drive into the main part of town, a solemn old citadel surrounded by cheap concrete houses and factories. The heart of it is heavy pale stone and, in the August stupor, empty of people. She takes his hand in the street, still enjoys the way he takes hers. They look in the closed shops and stop for coffee standing at the brass counter in an empty café, a clock ticking on the wall. She is silly with smiles. Gabriele walks beside her and sometimes is jovial, sometimes silent, sometimes does not smile as she teases him. He is newly grave, contained, impressive. A different person from the chubby cheery carpenter she had expected to see. He has shaved his chest, the line of fur is gone. The lines of his cheekbones are sharp and sublime. His reticence is unbearably erotic.

'How's the job?' she says, and he shrugs.

'You work so hard.'

Again, he is uninterested. 'I work. Don't be too impressed. Don't expect too much.'

But she is so happy with what she has.

She looks at him more than he does her. He used to be light; now he is serious. He no longer lifts her shrieking into the air; he looks at her with a quirked mouth and a thoughtful eye and says, 'You don't know how beautiful you are. My *tesoro*, my beautiful girl,' and kisses her neck to make the goosebumps rise.

There are reports on the news of people dying from heat. Her flesh inflates; it is all she can do to wear a light dress with bare legs, and free of winter clothes she feels untethered. Unsmiling, he runs his hand up her bare thigh. She shivers.

She knuckles herself into the bed. The room is full of their breath. Outside a morning church bell drones. In another room he is talking on the phone, talking to someone she doesn't know, in a murmured language that brushes meaning past her with unfamiliar, liquid verbs. She stretches, rolls luxuriously. Sucks the thought of him like a boiled lolly in her mouth. Come back to me. Now, now, now.

He comes back, tumbles her onto her belly, dives his face between her legs. She croons, helpless.

Later that afternoon they drive into Padua. There are people in the streets, and she is proud to be walking beside this gorgeous man, their matrimonial swagger. Her skin is damp and clear; she wets her face with cold water from a fountain. There is something voluptuous about the heat, of her pinned-up hair—long now—loosening in a damp scrawl against her neck. At the next fountain she palms water to his cheek, to cool it; she swings his hand and laughs; he smiles and says nothing.

Silence and glare of sun through clouds. They lie in the open of a great park—it is no cooler in the shade today. He rests her against him, holds her sticky heat close. He strokes her hair into place. His skin is green in its shadows. The trees sway but there is little breeze. She faces him, clear-eyed in the clear grey light, she lets him look at her closely, unafraid. His eyelids are drowsy, bruised to darkness.

'Let's go visit my friend,' he says, standing up. 'I've told her all about you. She's expecting us.'

She lets him pull her to her feet. 'A friend?'

They are busy in conversation even as she follows Gabriele into the kitchen. He walks straight to the fridge and swigs from a bottle of water. Donatella pretends not to notice her hesitation and her sweat, and hands her a welcome gift, a silver ring. 'I know you like silver,' she says in her high voice. They sit at the kitchen table and Donatella puts food on the table: olives, artichoke hearts, bread, a plastic bottle of water. She talks brightly, continuously, swinging her bleached blonde plaits over her shoulders again and again. There is a lot of leathery tanned skin to be seen; she wears only a midriff top, baring a muscled belly, shorts with a fringed belt, and a lot of silver jewellery. Her eyes are enormous, a weak blue. Her accent is strange, brittle and languid at the same time, she leaves the ending off words. 'I am *veneta*,' she says, 'lived here all my life.' She laughs a lot and watches Gabriele, who meets her gaze silent but amused.

'Katie, would you like to see some photos of me?'

An album is placed in her lap: studio photos of Donatella, wearing a cowboy hat, glossy lipstick, aviator sunglasses and no clothes. She glances at Gabriele. 'Have you seen these?' He shrugs. Donatella's breasts are small, polished and high, a young woman's breasts. She is forty-six years old.

'Lovely,' she says, not knowing what else to say.

'They're for my boyfriend,' Donatella says, caressing a page. 'He lives in Sicily, he's married.'

'Oh.' She sips her water. 'That must be difficult.'

'*Allora.*' Donatella is laughing. 'He is trouble. But I love him.'

Gabriele says something she can't catch. Donatella answers, some of the same words, more emphasised.

'Are you learning the local dialect?' she asks him.

'Trying to,' he says, and pokes an olive into Donatella's mouth. She laughs, shoves him with a brown hand, then bends to fix the strap of her beaded sandal; a glimpse of smooth brown breasts swinging loose beneath the turquoise top.

She sits there, docile, waiting to find the rhythm. She is glad Gabriele has a friend here, but this is not what she was expecting.

They stay for dinner, the inevitable pasta. Gabriele eats twice as much as the women. It's too hot. They idly twirl spaghetti on their forks. She leaves the chatting to the two of them, while she tries to catch the *veneta* accent; there are hints of French in its drawl and Donatella, even in Italian, has a dismissive lilt to everything she says. It occurs to her that the woman is nervous.

Gabriele switches on the television in the next room, they sit and watch a cable movie. It is an American film but dubbed in Italian. Everything is in Italian here. She is catching only a fraction of what is said. She stretches her arms over her head, makes herself look relaxed.

Near eleven Donatella disappears into another room.

'Can we leave soon?' she whispers. 'I want to fuck you.'

'We'll go right now. Out for ice-cream.'

She sits back, relieved. Donatella comes out, in a new outfit: still lots of skin, but cowboy boots and a short skirt. 'Ready,' she says. 'Ele, have you got money?'

They drive past black fields and closed factories to another small town; stroll through a great antique stone gate into a piazza the colour of wax under its streetlights. It is a huge open space, with a kiosk in the middle and many small tables where people are sitting. They take their place, peruse the menu. Gabriele and Donatella both decide on elaborate gelatos with candied fruit and whipped cream; she chooses sorbet and an espresso.

'Phew,' Donatella says, fanning herself. 'Hot, hot, hot.' She looks as if she were made for this: the slim arms, the tight skin so confidently bared. Gabriele wipes sweat from his face.

Donatella asks her about Australia, the men there, if they are all married, if they're any good.

'I don't remember,' she says, looking at Gabriele, 'I like Italians.'

'Ah yes,' says Donatella, rolling her eyes. 'But they are very *monello*.'

'*Monello*! Yes, that is exactly the word.'

She's tired. Jetlag. Heat. The effort of constant Italian. She drifts in and out of trying to follow their conversation; she admires Gabriele, so confident, here in his element. He catches her eye, makes a kissy mouth at her. She feels a little embarrassed for Donatella, as Gabriele catches her own finger and runs its tip along his bottom lip. He slips it into his mouth; his tongue is cold from ice-cream. She widens her eyes at him: *I want you*. The coffee makes her heart race.

'How many men have you been with?' Donatella wants to know. 'Have you had one-night stands? What kind of man do you prefer? What is the strangest thing you've ever done?' It is hard to answer in Italian but she tries. Donatella nods, sisterly. Gabriele interjects something; Donatella snaps back; the conversation gets away from her again. Her faltering remarks are lost.

She gazes along the line of yellow-lit sandstone walls to the black aperture of the city gate.

'Isn't it—' Donatella is turned to her now. 'For example, wouldn't it be transgressive to do something without an invitation?' she appeals. 'Like, kiss someone you hardly know?'

Gabriele, smiling, starts to interrupt; is shushed.

'It depends, whether—' she begins.

'You wouldn't do that, would you?' Gabriele says to Donatella. He gets a long, disdainful glare.

She blows smoke into the still air and waits to go home. But they drive back to Donatella's.

The television is still on; Donatella pulls a sofa out to make a bed and the three of them lie there, now, to watch music videos. The light from the screen flicks blue and purple in the dark room. Donatella mutters something; gets up and walks out.

Gabriele leans his face near to her ear. '*Tesoro. Tesoro.* Shall we play a trick on her?'

'What?' She is nearly asleep. 'A trick? Why?'

'You know how she was talking about transgressions. She looked so shocked at the idea. Why don't we show her? Why don't we,' and the blue light catches his sharp cat's tooth, 'seduce her?'

She stares at him, confused. Why? What a silly trick. She likes Donatella well enough, she doesn't want to play tricks. What would be the point? This is not what she came here for. She's never been with a woman before. Donatella is much more trim than she is, she'd be embarrassed. 'Can't we just go home?'

'No, it'll be good. She needs some fun. We will teach her something. Come on.' He puts his hand around her jaw, lifts it to kiss her. They are still kissing when Donatella comes back and settles down on the bed next to them.

Gabriele turns to her.

I don't want to, she thinks, as he whispers in Donatella's ear. She watches as Donatella's eyes widen, then blink, as Gabriele takes her face and kisses her gently on the lips.

Donatella turns her eyes to her. 'Katie?'

'Don't be scared, it's okay,' she says. 'We thought you might like to try something new.'

Gabriele slips the shoulder strap off Donatella's brown skin, and kisses the round bone there. The woman doesn't move. She reaches over, tentatively strokes Donatella's shin, then Gabriele's hip. Perhaps Donatella felt lonely, seeing them together. Her own lover so far away in Sicily.

'No, no, Ele,' Donatella gasps as he slides his weight on top of her. But she sighs and flattens against the sheet, her arm pulls him in closer.

She slips off her dress. She is ready when Gabriele turns and engulfs her in his arms, when another hand slides up her leg, her mouth is open and when she sighs it is part acquiescence, part pleasure, part astonishment.

+

In the creepy lustre of the television screen and the hot darkness, their bodies are sculpted by shadows. Skin soapy with sweat, mouths dry with breath and wet with kisses. Donatella's flesh is unfamiliar and soft under her hesitant hands; she keeps to limbs and face, while Gabriele plunges here and there. A rhythm comes over them: he alternately kisses and fingers each woman. Hands grip, skin slips, fits.

His body is buried in hers, his mouth in Donatella's. He is a fulcrum for both.

A desperate kiss, her hair falling damply on his face.

The strong lines of his jaw as he kisses the other woman.

Her own pleasure is a thin veil; she pulls it from her skin and watches them all. Pride pulses up in her, more luxurious than pleasure; *You're mine*, she mouths at him over Donatella's shoulder. He returns a drugged glance, a long secret look; opens his mouth; she comes to him.

When Donatella reaches orgasm their hands grip, small strong bones clutching. She strokes blonde hair wet as seaweed from the woman's face, sweat from his flank.

Gabriele whispers something in the other woman's ear, smirking; she retorts, her voice sharp after the soft moaning; he replies. And suddenly Donatella covers her face with her hands, scrambles to her feet, leaves the room.

'I don't understand,' she says. 'Did we scare her?'

'Shh,' he says and slides himself into her, that familiar taking, her hands reaching for his hips without thought. In the sweaty slither he arches and bucks, his mouth muffled against her hair.

They quieten. She has not come, she is not willing enough. She's waiting to understand.

✦

They lie on either side of Donatella. Honesty is in the air. Donatella smooths her hand. 'Katie, I think I've hurt you,' she says.

'Hurt me?' She is sleepy, perplexed. It must be five in the morning. The woman waits; closes her eyes, nestles down further. Gabriele's hand lies on Donatella's belly, stroking small circles. 'No, it was okay, I wanted to.'

'How do you feel about him?' Donatella opens her eyes. 'Tell me truly. I'm curious. You're so free.'

The effort to keep understanding the language is almost too much. 'I am in love with him,' she says. That is easy to say. *Innamorata di lui.* 'It's always joy, simplicity.' The words she has used so often to him, in emails, a vocabulary of emotions. *Tenerezza, dolcezza.* 'I think he's good, I think he's honest. Tender. I've waited a long time.' Smiling across her to his silhouette in the dark.

'Ele,' Donatella says, impassive as a fortune–teller, 'And tell me, how do you feel? No, you have to speak more slowly. She can't follow. She wants to know. She needs to.'

Thank god for Donatella, she thinks. She is kind.

He mumbles.

'Do you love her? Yes or no?'

Quiet.

More quiet.

'Yes,' he says, 'yes. I love her.'

They fall asleep at dawn, day's warmth already scalding the cracks of the drawn shutters, hands thrown across shoulders, brushing breasts.

✦

At noon they have breakfast together (coffee, made strong, Napoletano style, and hard sugary biscuits). The metal shutters are drawn down as tightly as possible and they move as if underwater in the gloom. Heat makes them quiet and heavy; her dress from yesterday stinks. Donatella beckons her into the bedroom, invites her to borrow something. The other woman is half her size but she finds a long elasticised cotton skirt and a tight low-cut peasant top; Donatella wreathes a fancy belt loosely around her hips; it is a style she has never worn. She sways the skirt, pleased, and Donatella says, 'Like an Italian. *Brava.*'

They go out. It seems they are going shopping. They park outside a huge plaza in the middle of bare fields: she didn't know such things existed in Italy. Airconditioning soothes them as they enter. It feels very normal, as they flick absently through racks of clothes. The women suggest shirts for Gabriele, hold them up against him, agree on what suits. Her legs bounce the fabric of the long skirt with every step, she feels jaunty now she's not stupefied by heat. Her bared hips are lean with sex.

Donatella gives her complicit looks, woman to woman; on the escalator Gabriele kisses her deeply, pinches Donatella's arse as they walk along. Respectable couples sneak looks. She feels wonderful.

But when they return to Donatella's apartment she grows quiet.

Donatella's apartment, a shopping centre, a piazza for coffee, Gabriele's house. That is all there is here. After Rome, it seems a life bleached of colour. She dawdles as they walk ahead of her into the dim flat, and wonder how they can bear it.

✦

In the twilit doorway of the balcony they sit, getting a little breeze. Donatella has gone to have a nap. They are quiet, solemn. A dog is barking moronically, on and on, caught somewhere. She holds his hand, her thumb rubbing one knuckle over and over.

'This is a bad place,' she says. 'I can feel it. There's nothing here. It's empty. You were happy in Rome. You're so different now.'

His eyes are huge. He closes them.

'You don't agree?'

'I agree,' he says. 'I know.' His face is very still.

She dares speak on. 'All this time I've been thinking of you, *tesoro*. All this time hoping you're okay. I missed you so much. You know I went home because I had to, you knew that. Not to leave you behind. I'm sorry.' She traces circles on his knee. 'I can't explain anything properly, I don't have the words, forgive me, *tesoro*. Maybe I've changed a bit but I still love you. I love you so.' She hesitates. 'I don't know who you are now—you're different and you're more beautiful. I'm scared—'

He picks up her hand, presses it against his cheek.

'I know it's been a hard time. You always have to work so hard. I've been waiting to hold you again, and now I'm here and it's all I want—'

His cheek is cool with tears as he crouches in her arms.

He says nothing at all. She holds him, fearful, hushing him, murmuring that it is all okay.

+

The sex that night is lighter, friendlier. A trio now, they already have an understanding. But she lies there, bored, wanting only privacy with Gabriele. She protests her sleepiness, becomes passive. They roll her into their embrace, tug her into place; Donatella runs fingers through her hair and when she reaches up, finally, her own fingers find flesh easy beneath them. For the first time she presses her mouth against Donatella's, finds it softer than she expected, kisses deeper. She is pleased, after all. Turn and turn about; they share their chances, take them; Gabriele twists from one to another. They tumble and caress, reaching hands where they will fit, snaking beneath arms, between legs, two hands meeting in the one place. They all taste of each other.

+

She stirs, and wakes. Her heart is sounding slow and sure against Gabriele's side. His face is turned to Donatella's. The two of them are talking low, Gabriele's hand absentmindedly smoothing her own thigh.

She can't move; she's adhered to him with sweat. Her body is far away, she's barely there at all. They have probably slept a long time. What delicious stillness.

Whispers. Gabriele's breathing is even. As she starts to remember to translate, she hears him say, 'You know how I feel.'

Donatella replies, something too hushed to catch. She hears him say, 'When we made love last week.'

Surely he must feel her heart against his skin. It has tripped and fallen.

Quietly she lies there. They talk on. Words scatter past. She is too full of oxygen, she can't breathe. Can't he feel it, that she has stopped breathing? She can't catch her heartbeat.

Move, she thinks. Fucking *move*.

In the bathroom, whitely naked, she gasps for air. Something stings: salt, or blood returning to a dead limb. How alone she feels. I don't believe it, I don't believe it, she chants.

Or was she expecting this? Something feels familiar.

She is fish-mouthed in the mirror, gaping.

Running into the living room she yanks on clothes. She mustn't let them catch her. There is no fucking air in this apartment. Haul up the shutters enough to scuttle, fast as she can, to the refuge of the balcony. She drags on a cigarette and her hands chatter. Stupid, stupid, they think I'm fucking stupid, I am so stupid. *Fuck.*

Gabriele settles on the balcony, next to the shutter, wordless. Her stare trembles out over the dry street, the dull concrete houses opposite, the tired dying trees. The sky is grey. She squints at him in the glare. His eyes are troubled, the pupils small. He looks at her. She turns her face away. Her mouth opens; words start to stutter from the fragments in her head.

'You *stronzo*, you arsehole, you think I'm such a stupid foreigner, you thought—you thought I was an idiot—I can't—' Her hands fly out, make gestures, slash the air, pointless. She's gasping.

How she hates this language. Breathe. 'You and she—'

'Yes,' he says.

She thinks: *No.* Does she actually recoil?

'I told you not to expect too much of me,' he says. 'On the second day here I told you.'

He is murky, green eyes, khaki skin. All the colour and

gleam have gone. Her cigarette: she smokes and smokes.

Silence and heat.

'You let me come here. You let me think—thought—that I was still your girl. You said you don't—didn't—hide anything.' She fumbles the tense of the verb. All the tenses are wrong.

'I've hidden a lot from you.' His voice is so quiet.

She is frightened. This man she doesn't know at all.

How shapeless he is, all the lean definition gone. His mouth is swollen. He's squashed with a kind of resignation. He is not going to apologise. There is a terrible beaten, defensive look in his eyes.

'Yes,' she says narrowly.

'I've had more troubles than you know. You've been far away. My feelings changed. I think,' he says, 'I think I'm in love with her.'

Her. *Lei*. Such an elegant word. She loathes it.

'*Her*,' she says slowly. 'I don't give a fuck about *her*.' She flicks her fingers beneath her chin with contempt. The correct gesture. '*You*, you've made me feel—'

Ash from the cigarette falls on her. 'I've been here four days and all this time—'

She has not the words to ask why. Already she is exhaling. She is a soggy lung. Already she knows. Gabriele's miserable eyes, only his quiet mouth not unsaying anything. She throws the unfinished cigarette over the edge. They sit, fatigued, on the hot balcony. It is nine o'clock in the morning.

+

'Do you want to talk to me?'

Donatella shakes her head, her face hidden in her hands, and cries harder.

Her tongue is sealed against her palate. She watches

Gabriele crouch over Donatella, their intimate syllables crooning, their stupid language. She and Gabriele were halfway down the stairs when he said, 'Wait, I think she's crying.' He disappeared back into the apartment. 'She feels bad,' he said, coming back. She stared at him as he went back in, and sat on the tiled steps a minute more.

She went into the dim rooms, the powdery scent of furniture polish. The stale air. The ugly Italian furnishings.

'I don't hate you, Donatella,' she says flatly. How could she hate her? So little, her brave face grown old, sobbing into her hands.

*Slut.*

'I know you didn't mean to hurt me.' She glares at Gabriele. In English she mutters, 'This is my fucking moment, you bastard.' He strokes Donatella's arms while she sits and wraps herself tighter.

She takes off the big silver ring Donatella gave her; what would a local girl do? Hurl it back at her? It could do some damage. She puts it in her pocket instead. Oh, how ridiculous. She is wearing Donatella's clothes.

Something strange is happening; more and more air is filling her. It is horror. Her chest is straining. This is happening. She speaks out, hard puffs of pain.

'I just—you let me come here, and all your friends knew I was coming, the stupid foreigner, and I thought you wanted me and I'm not—they all *know*—'

The thought of whispering *You're mine*, while he fucked her.

'—and—'

Wretched tears gush. She does feel something. And now I have to go home without even the dream of you, Gabriele.

He paces towards her now, his voice husky, defensive, gasps

215

rising. She can't understand what he's saying. Platinum sheen of tears on his face in the grey dim air. She sits like a pebble, just looking.

'What was I to do, I was—should I have called you? Called you, and said, Don't come? I thought it was—and you abandoned me, you left me, I'm always abandoned, I waited—I *loved* you—'

His fingers bunched, pleading, raised. He is before her now, he flicks his fingers hard against her shoulder as he did once before; she turns her face away. Sweat goes on dampening her dress as he walks to the window. A rushing stream of words, words she can't follow, words she's never learned. But she understands the breaking of his voice; she understands Donatella sitting very still on the other couch; she understands Donatella saying sharply, 'Ele, Ele, keep your voice down, don't—' as he starts to wail, starts to keen in grief.

He is coming undone in front of them. 'I've been trying for so long—*so long*, always trying—'

His cracked howl weighs them in their places.

But when he starts to sob the two women walk to him, wrap their arms about his shudders. They weep with him. They press him back into solidity.

The air trembles down again.

They sit, the three of them crumpled together on one seat. Their faces are stiff with tears. Donatella makes small cups of strong coffee.

With dreamy water-bound thoughts, she recognises it all; she won't fight. She leans against Donatella and they both look at him with tear-tight eyes.

Just one syllable, one vowel. The verb changes. I love you. I loved you. You love her.

If she hadn't concentrated, she might have missed it. If

she hadn't learned Italian. *Hai capito? Hai capito?* Yes, she'd murmured, I understand, even when she hadn't.

It wasn't the dark that frightened her, it was the fear of the unseen step in it, a drop, a plummeting, a loss.

'I want to go home now,' she says. 'Can we just go home?'

✦

In his kitchen the shutters have been closed for two days. The heat sinks around her, compresses her into shape. She showers, scrubs her skin, steps out fresh. She puts on a pink silk slip and no underwear, lies down on the bed. He looks dazed. A miserable boy.

Grief starts to seep through her, as if her blood is congealing, vein by vein. It is a calm sensation. She is impressed with her calmness. He gazes at her, with soft baby eyes. She sips from a bottle of water, her limbs pale in the light.

'You won't forget me.'

'I couldn't,' he says.

She remembers Jack saying to her tear-stained face, *I don't flog dead horses.* She's not that girl now.

The afternoon passes. They lie on the bed, watch television, she dozes, her head on his shoulder. They haven't yet learned how not to do that. He makes love to her later, his face dreamlike with feeling, her eyes insistently open: she watches him, her lost prize.

He goes out to ring his parents from a phonebox, though he has a mobile. He is gone two hours. They are together, she knows, and does not let herself cry. She sprawls in the long dusk drinking water on the landing, smoking and listening to the dogs' twilight frenzy. Church bells, neighbourhood women emerging to gossip over their fences, female voices calling kids home. Children ride past on scooters. The moon is rising in powdery blue light. Her dreams of this land are over. Well, she'll go home free now. *You are so free.* Deep pulses of grief become a rhythm, a warm ache. It is tasty as salt. She finds herself almost happy.

He comes up the stairs to find her watching the moon. He kisses her, nuzzles his warm face against hers, murmurs something bashful, something sweet. His smiles are easy now.

His phone rings, he hands it straight to her to answer. 'Katie. Would you like to come out later with me?' Donatella's voice is shy, she speaks slowly, to be understood.

'Yes.' she says. 'I'd like that. Can Gabriele come too?'

The cool of dusk quickens the blood. Gabriele holds her hand. In the kitchen he cooks her spaghetti with his old jokes. They watch a corny variety show and as the end credits roll to a showtune he pulls her to him. And they sway to the silly old song.

+

Something new begins.

The three of them go out every night, at midnight. They dress up; she feels beautiful, her flesh eased by touching, her eyes luminous. Her skin fits better, they fit together, lovers all three. *Tutti e tre.* They drive past the black fields to a different town each night, joking or silent together, music loud in the car's plush cabin. Gabriele sings along badly; under her breath, she joins in. They walk through empty antique streets, below porticoes, sit for coffee in bone-coloured piazzas among couples. The nights are quiet, the squares full of people strolling, released from the captivity of the day.

They talk, mock, commiserate, sing, swing each other's hands. She catches his eye, he winks.

'What do you know about anything, idiot?' Donatella snaps at him, and he kisses her hand.

He throws his arms around their shoulders, they learn to walk at the same pace. Donatella throws her arms up and clasps her by the shoulders, small and fervent. 'Did you see them looking at us?' Donatella says happily. It feels like everyone is looking at them, in envy.

She teaches them words in English: *blow job, get fucked, dick-head*. Donatella takes up smoking again; Gabriele lights their cigarettes, takes a puff himself. They eat enormous gelati, stuck with fruit slices and fluffy with cream, placing wet spoonfuls in each other's sugary mouths. Two o'clock in the morning, time for another coffee. They walk slowly, through humid ochre streets and past bleached walls made to keep enemies out. The moon is always above, the planets burning.

She waves her cigarette in the air, joins them peering into dark shop windows. He tells jokes and the language swims more fluidly than ever through her mind; she understands how funny he is, how confident. They are all together, happy, so happy. They drive home in the indigo dark to make love; she sits in the back of the car, thoughts flickering dark and light, wind filling her mouth.

✦

'When will you leave?' he asks her in the afternoon silence of a piazza.

'When you want me to.' She won't let the lurch of her heart spoil the happiness. 'Tomorrow. Do you want me to leave tomorrow?'

He shrugs. Smiles. She stays.

*Try north, somewhere nice like Tuscany...*

The conversation about the future never happens. She never mentions the box packed at home, to be sent on. Here she wears the same clothes, washed and folded by Gabriele every day, and her bag stays unpacked on his bedroom floor. Perhaps she should leave, surely she should leave. In a way she looks forward to picking up that bag again; just passing through, after all. But she's too sleepy.

Back at his house she lies down next to him. For the first time she hesitates to touch him alone. She needs permission. He takes her hand and places it. She finds herself laughing just as she always had.

Their bodies swing, meet, adhere; separate, meet again.

+

In the bathroom she washes her hands. She remembers cooling herself in a fountain, laughing, the day they went to meet Donatella.

Why didn't she just leave after that first fight—flounce to pack her bag, demand a lift to the station? She's never flounced off anywhere in her life. She's too stupid.

And where would she have gone? A forlorn figure, standing on a platform, watching her boyfriend walk back to his mistress. The great, annihilating, decision-sapping heat. Herself, becoming only a shimmer in the haze on her way to nowhere.

Soon it will be the afterwards. The terrible alone afterwards of her love for Gabriele.

The tears are not cool, they are hot and sour. It feels as if she has been scooped empty from sorrow. Her throat opens and the dreadful world plunges down it.

There will be no more returns to Italy now. No more emails from him to make her giggle in Melbourne. He will not raise his head beaming to greet her at another train station. The Gabriele baby will not be born; all the warm water of love has sluiced from her. She will go back to Melbourne, to explain, and it will all be over.

Because she did not understand, she did not follow.

✦

She scrambles through the gap like a creature, and squats on Donatella's balcony, naked under her dress. The air is rust on her skin, in her throat, so hot. She blinks dry eyes. She smokes, her iron-railed square a refuge from the kitchen table conversation inside, from all the words she still doesn't know. They are saying more with their eyes than with their lips again.

She sucks in hot dry smoke, blows it into hot dry air.

The street below is empty but for a tanned old man, shirtless, riding a bicycle in slow motion. The bells of a church tower sing dolefully over the concrete houses, the dusty gardens. She touches herself beneath the dress, testing. Her cunt is moist and hot. The rest of her is dry. She chucks the cigarette over the railing.

Inside, Gabriele is sitting alone in the living room.

'Come here, beautiful,' he says. Then a brilliant grin. She smooths her hair, her sexy hair that is full of sweat and caresses. 'You smoke a lot. Are you nervous?'

'There's nothing else to do,' she says, walking over.

'*Tesoro*,' he whispers, 'my *tesoro*.'

Don't say that, she thinks. Don't you feel me flinch? Those names aren't right anymore.

He smiles a little sadly. She kisses his neck, licks the salt off him. He squeezes her, goes to look for Donatella in the bedroom. Donatella is not well, the heat is not good for her.

The tense sweep of her arm raising the cigarette, that's her strength now. Her victory. She will not smash the room, she will not plead, she will not scream.

✦

He comes to her in the dimness of Donatella's bedroom a little later. The other woman has gone out for groceries. She is laying out the washed clothes: the lovely long skirt, the delicate top that made her feel pretty. She makes herself lay them down gently, not throw them in a heap.

'I hurt you. Can you forgive me?' he says. His arms are hot and heavy around her waist. 'I love her. But you are also the one I love, just not the same as before. Now that you are here. You will always be my *tesoro*.' He kisses her. This kiss might have been different. They might have fucked all afternoon. Except that her arms are tense, resting along his. Except that it is not their bed.

She looks at him; her mouth won't smile. I don't trust you, I don't trust you, she thinks. 'Okay, Gabriele. Sure.'

She extricates herself from his embrace. She has looked up the Italian for 'liar', for 'misunderstand', for 'deceive'. 'Tell me, Gabriele,' she says. 'How long have you been with Donatella?' *I heard you talking, I heard you.*

'We've cried together,' he says. 'She has been with me when I cried.'

'When you two were talking. In bed. That morning. You said you had sex last week.' In the wardrobe mirror she sees him from the back: lean, desirable, his dark round head tilted to one side. She's always despised the backs of people's heads.

'Not us,' he says. 'I was talking about her and the other guy. The Sicilian. He was here last week.'

He waits. 'You're still angry?'

'No,' she says, defeated, 'I'm not angry. Just hot.'

'You want to fight with me? Here,' he says, 'hit me.'

'I want to smash something.' But her voice is dry.

'Hit me, it won't matter. I'll hit you back,' he says mischievously. Her face is numb, and her body arches away from him minutely. She raises her hand. She imagines its feeble blow. Her dull useless ire.

'No,' she says. 'I don't want to fight.'

She is thinking: I'd like to slash you open and crawl inside. I want to pare you with blades.

She stands there, a stiff doll, helpless. 'It's okay, Ele. I forgive you.'

*Perdonare, perdere.* In Italian, 'to forgive' is nearly the same as 'to lose'.

+

Gabriele runs into the living room that night. 'Come and help me. She's not well.'

She finds the small woman propped on the floor against the side of the bed. Donatella is an unpleasant colour in the lamplight; she draws in breath shuddering, her eyes closed. Without opening them, she says, 'Don't worry, Katie. I'm okay. *Tutto bene. Tutto bene.*'

'What's wrong?' she asks Gabriele.

He kneels beside Donatella, wipes the hair off her brow.

'Tachycardia. Her heart.' He mimes it fluttering. 'She's not well.'

'I'm fine,' Donatella whispers. 'I just have to take it easy.'

She doesn't know what to do. Gabriele is absorbed, murmuring to Donatella, his face drawn. She backs off, unwilling to look heartless, uneasy with staying. 'Should we call a doctor?'

'I've had my pills, just need to rest,' Donatella says. She swallows. 'My heart isn't so strong, Katie.' She opens her eyes and looks up; it's unbearable. 'Not so strong after all, the bastard.' She chuckles weakly.

'Keep quiet,' Gabriele says, and blows on her face gently, his own skin shining with anxiety.

'Your heart is strong enough,' she assures Donatella, as she backs out of the room.

+

In the late morning she and Donatella loll naked on the sofa bed and share girl-talk. They giggle, snort, they labour through language to chat.

'You know, *cara*, loving men is hard,' Donatella says.

'Oh Dolly, I know.'

'I've given a lot in my time. You too, I think. You still love him very much, don't you?'

Donatella loves her Sicilian, whom she can't have, and she loves Gabriele, and he loves both of us, we are all trying so hard.

'I'll always love him. But he's not mine anymore.'

They stare at each other. 'He probably has another five girls somewhere else,' Donatella says, 'no wonder he's tired,' and they burst into laughter. They quieten, stick their feet in the air, idly swing them towards each other.

Gabriele passes through the room, flicks an amused look at them.

*Loving men is hard.* In this same hemisphere, this same country, she has known many men. Massimo. His diabolical grin flashes into her mind. Oh, Massimo and Nanni and Guido, how long ago that feels, those mad days. Jack, poor old Jack. All the others. Lessons, lessons. She folds her knees to her chest, sighs. Too complicated to explain to Donatella in Italian, after all. She encloses them within, her secrets. They won't ever leave her.

She gets up and corners him in the kitchen; he scoops coffee-drenched sugar from the cafetière onto her tongue with his fingers, crams them into her mouth; she is unstrung with the sweetness. Caffeine and sugar crackle into her system along with desire.

She finds herself staring at him all the time. Is it possible that he is becoming more beautiful? She makes herself walk out of the room.

She opens the bathroom door, her face sluiced with tears. Gabriele and Donatella are standing there together, naked under the shower, faces cupped in each other's hands. She is interrupting. They had all been in bed, a greasy morning tangle and then she had started crying. They hadn't noticed, mashed up in each other. She had cried while they made love, a small figure on the edge of the bed, and then they were getting up and walking away to the bathroom and she had cried more and then couldn't stand being alone.

'Come in, in here,' they say. 'Come in, Katie.' Her name is strange in their accent. She steps blindly into the bathtub, under the water. They enclose her. With tender silky hands they wash her body, smoothing soap, anointing her with water.

She leans her face to the tiles and tears continue weeping down her face. Her body shudders. The water makes sounds to hush her.

'Did you think we were making love in here without you?' Gabriele says. He rinses her face with a palmful of water.

'I heard breathing, hard breathing. You were fucking without me.'

'We heard you scream on the other side of the door. You said *fuck!*' They giggle at the word in English.

'But it was me, *tesoro*,' he says, 'I was crying. I was crying too.' His face is flushed.

Donatella leaves them, a trailing hand cool on her flank.

The water is turned off. A thin light comes through the fogged window. They step out of the bath and he takes a towel and begins to dry her. She is limp, resigned as a child.

She breathes in. 'I'm not crying because I'm sad. I was crying because I saw you together on the bed and you were so beautiful.'

She thinks of Donatella's glances at her over his firm safe arms. Their two faces close on the bed, the brown skin wrapped tight, their intimate easy laughter as she watched. 'You're both so kind to me.' He stops drying her. His hands hold the towel in the air. He looks away and she sees his eyes cloudy with fatigue and feeling, the blood pink in his cheeks. 'It's all right, Gabriele. I'll be all right. You know I love you. I want you to be happy.'

Moisture beads on their skin. He is crying, as quietly as she.

'You know,' he says, 'that's what Donatella said to me. That first night. She'd never seen people look at each other like we did, as we looked that first night when we were making love. That's why she cried.'

There is a bruise on her nipple, she sees. She doesn't know whose teeth left it there.

Which of them can afford to be generous today?

+

She takes photographs: Gabriele stepping naked from a shower, almost bashful; their three smiles, eyes crescented, too close to the camera; Donatella and she, faces flushed and hair damp with sweat crushing their lips together. Gabriele gleefully biting Donatella's thigh.

In the furred bathroom light she points the camera to herself, does not pose, only stares. Her own face, blurred, the flush of this strange summer on her skin, eyes humid and mouth steady. She washes the morning's juice from her, the salty scent all over like an anointment, and when she enters the room he is back between Donatella's legs. She lies down and kisses the blonde head, strokes his shorn one.

'It's her turn now, Ele,' Donatella says. He shifts over, settles his face warm between her own legs. A small hand fits over her breast. 'You like that, *cara*? We want you to feel good, I want you to feel beautiful, you are my beautiful friend,' Donatella says. 'A *principessa*,' says Gabriele. She shakes her head; but lies back. She feels like a body under the knife. Donatella whispers hot damp air into her ear, Gabriele's mouth sucks and teases; one hand in Donatella's, one flexing in his. She squirms in gratitude, but then, 'It's Dolly's turn again now,' she says, and gently disengages.

+

He says, 'Come on, let's go to Australia when she leaves. We can go for a week. All together. *Tutti e tre*. It will be wonderful there.'

'Oh yes,' says Donatella. 'All three. I would like that.'

They go home to his place in the afternoon, leaving Donatella to have her nap, and lie on the big bed. 'Come here, closer,' he says, as he always had. Warmth makes their skin translucent. 'About coming to Australia,' she says, afraid even to hope. 'You're just dreaming. It's just a dream.'

'I'm allowed to dream,' he says sharply.

Her dreams had been of afternoons like this when they reunited, of slow sex and sweat and swollen mouths. She runs fingers down his arm, the damp silky skin. She stares in wonder at each tiny stick of stubble on his jaw, the tiny lines around his eyes. He is real. He sleeps, heavy flesh, one big knuckled hand resting on her as light as a kiss.

227

She learns his skin all over again, with a kind of awe.

A single bird drones; in her mind she feels a door-latch spring open, something ease. She puts his hand aside, gets up, smokes in the kitchen. Time is slow. She is thinner already. It is almost done.

✦

'Go to her,' he says in the dark living room on the last night. 'She's half in love with you, make love to her. I think she's sad.'

'In love with me?' This is a surprise. 'I doubt it.' She thinks of Donatella on the bed, alone. Would you like the night alone with him, *cara*, the other woman had said, and removed her little lithe body.

In the darkness of the bedroom she touches Donatella's shoulder. She leaps.

'Oh. I was asleep.'

She sits down. 'Donatella, are you lonely? Come in with us.'

The light snaps on and the other woman faces her very straight in the lamplight. 'Katie, you don't have to do that.' They look at each other. 'I am sorry,' her blue eyes so pale, 'for all of this.'

'It's okay. I'm sorry too.' She strokes Donatella's arm. 'Look after yourself. Look after him for me when I'm gone.'

'He always talked of you, *cara*, of his Australian girl. When we made love, he and I, we were always crying. It was our solitudes that were touching; we made love crying. He loves you.'

'I don't know. He used to. I don't know who he loves now.'

'We love each other, don't we. We all love each other.'

They kiss each other goodnight on the cheek, and the light goes off again.

✦

He makes love to her in the doorway open to the night. How beautiful his face is. He pushes in and looks down at her; it is as if everything were as simple as light and shadow, dark and bright.

She reaches up her arms, and brings him down to her.

✦

She finds Gabriele curled on the bed the next day. She has been on the balcony. When she touches his shoulder he rolls over and his eyes are wet. 'Katie,' he says.

'*Tesoro*. Don't be sad. I'm not sorry I came to see you.' She runs her fingers over his tears, strokes them away. 'But I have to leave.'

'You were right,' he says. 'Dolly and I. We were together before you came. Not long before,' he says, pleading. 'Not long.'

The room is so dim, so safe. 'I know.'

'I'm sorry. I'm sorry.'

'It's all right.'

'I was lonely. And I was sad. We were both so sad. I missed you so much.'

'Shh.'

He pulls a ring off his hand, a thick band of silver. 'This is for you.' He manages a smile. 'So you never forget me.'

'I couldn't.' She puts the ring on the same hand as Donatella's. Holds her hand out to show him. 'See? I take you both with me.'

Of course she does. Nothing will be the same again.

✦

At the kitchen table she says, 'I have a present for you. In exchange for the ring.'

'No, no,' says Donatella, beaming.

229

She comes to stand near, so tall over this small woman. She kisses her cheek. 'This is for your sweetness.' Another kiss. 'This for your beauty. This for your sadness. And this,' taking a string of leather with a silver pendant from her own throat, 'is for your memories.'

Gabriele is watching. She expands the loop, puts it on Donatella, pulls it into place. But the knot catches, snarls, digs into the soft throat, the leather snags and can't be loosened. It is choking her. It is not what she intended.

+

That night they pack the car. The holiday is over; his house will fill again; there is no room for her. It is time. These are the last hours together. They will take her to Rome; they will do that for her, to keep her as long as possible. She sits in the back with the windows open. They set off at ten; they will drive all night.

The music is on. They shoot south for a couple of hours; stop at a drive-through and drink coffee. Back in the car. More driving, more hours; she sleeps a while, wakes up and they stop for more coffee; drive on. It is four in the morning.

She and Gabriele reminisce; they tell Donatella of their first meeting, the bum-shaped hollow on the car bonnet, the way she'd been so suspicious of him, the sudden kiss by the fountain. She leans forward, she has her arms loosely around his shoulders, they are laughing, warm and nostalgic; Donatella is laughing too.

'Has anyone ever done that to you, Dolly? Just met you and kissed you like a *monello*?' She squeezes Gabriele's shoulder.

'Actually,' Donatella says, fondly, 'the first night I met Gabriele. After he'd just arrived in Padua. We went out with his friends and he kissed me and he said, "When's the last time you were kissed by a man my age?"'

She disengages from Gabriele. Sits back. In the warm

rushing air she is shimmering, tiny frozen sparks stuttering her blood.

'Tell me all about it,' she says. Six months. He moved up here six months ago.

They are on the freeway, cars speeding past, changing lanes, lights streaming backwards, the wind bashing in through the windows. They are going too fast, they are speeding through the dark.

'Gabriele,' she says, 'tell me all about it, go on. You know, Donatella,' she continues, since Gabriele will not meet her eye in the mirror and he is driving now with locked arms, 'I'm interested, because I asked him about it and he lied, and then this morning he told me—the fucking—the fucking *bastard*—'

But they are nearly in the city, where they will say goodbye, and it doesn't matter anymore.

He is just a boy, after all. And she, she was a liar once, too. How much sweeter it is to forgive weakness, than despise it.

'I don't care,' she says tiredly. 'You're an arsehole, but never mind. You didn't need to lie to me. I love you both,' she says. 'It doesn't matter.'

Donatella is sitting very small and quiet in the front seat. Gabriele starts to say something; chokes.

The wind is in her ears, she can't hear him. She breathes in the hot rushing air, the sirocco. Music fills the car; she lays her hands on their shoulders and they lean in, sing together. The silence and the blackness fall away as they hurtle on.

✦

They reach the city just before dawn. Tottering with tiredness they get out and walk empty streets and piazzas stage-lit for no one, their grandeur weirdly artificial. The sheened light of dawn seeps across the sky, pink and yellow. Donatella trails behind, blinking, as they hold hands and remember their times here. The city hasn't changed. They recall where they made love; where they ate and bought coffees. The Spanish Steps, the Capitoline, piazza Navona. Campo de' Fiori. The fountain where they first kissed is running in the empty piazza. They kiss there now. They take photographs of each other in pairs, lit by the flash against shadowy entrances, vacant steps.

They park the car near her hotel and sleep for an hour in it, awkwardly crumpled. They wake to rotten sunshine and swollen skin. Donatella opens the door and gets out to sit on the gutter.

'Come here, *tesoro*,' he says, and she gets into the front. He pulls her onto him, cradles her for the last time; they doze. She wants to remember his arms holding her, the exact dimensions of his chest. Before she can cry she gets out, flinches in the sunlight, goes to sit next to Donatella and lights a cigarette. She is creaky with sadness.

Music starts in the car. It is Gabriele, opening the doors to let it out, tipping water from a bottle over his sleek head, looking up in a shower of sparkling drops. He grins at her, brown and bright, more beautiful than she can bear; just the way he once looked at her beside a wall in Circus Maximus.

Donatella clutches her as she sobs and sobs, the cigarette turning to crushed ash.

He pulls her to her feet when she's finished, when she's exhausted, and holds his arms out to dance. She stumbles into step, lays her head on his shoulder. They sway sweetly, slowly. Under the umbrella pines she twirls, and he catches her.

The end, the dreaded last moments, are gentle. She is nauseous with fatigue; the street goes dark for a moment as she looks up at the awful morning sunshine.

'Don't cry anymore,' they say. 'Don't cry now.'

Donatella holds her arms up, she crushes the little bones briefly, they smile at each other.

'Goodbye, *cara*, I wish you well.'

'I hope you return one day,' Donatella says. 'Come back, come back to us.' She gets in the car.

She watches Gabriele coming towards her, the creases of soft skin at his throat, his crooked tooth, the black fleck in one iris, his wide smile. She is used to him.

'Don't be sad,' he says, wreathing her with his heavy arms. 'Don't ever be afraid.'

In a moment he's gone. She watches them drive away. This is the city where they met; they have said goodbye here before.

'You are in my heart,' he had said.

'You are my heart,' she replied.

But her heart is gone. She was always trying to give it away.

part seven

# KATE

*I am not now*
*That which I have been.*
**BYRON**

The city closes around her like a familiar hand; she has returned. It is August and the air is hotter than the blood of the body.

The first morning, she walks the narrow streets of the *centro*. Empty, echoing, abandoned for summer, they are all hers. The old city has remained the same all these years without her: perhaps a little more graffiti, new rubbish in the seams, the peach and rose ochre only a little more faded, yet the ruins are no more ruined than in her time.

When she arrives at each corner there is a moment when she startles, to find herself lost; then steadies, because she has walked these streets times beyond number and her body takes the turn as easily as moving in her own skin.

She walks towards the darkened window of a shop; her reflection flickers there. Sweet and strange, to think that this reflection has been absent; to think she ever imagined it might linger.

The Shelley museum is open again these days, years after its renovations, but closed for the month. She looks in at Byron's doorway, up at the window of the Goethe house. The lines have dissolved in her memory: she can only remember *He has outsoared the shadow of our night…*

Weighing down her handbag, one of her old diaries and a notebook.

At the Forum, she has to pay to enter and even more of the

grounds are closed to the public. Rome is again barricading against invaders. Oblivious, the ruins rest the blunt pads of their paws on the grass.

A single column hangs in the middle of the dry air, its edges nibbled and frail. The column was set up in the last days of the empire, when they had forgotten how to make a column; they took it from its cousins and pretended it was new. The Romantics admired it for the loneliness, the poignancy. It stands singular, brave, dazzled.

Someone has been hosing down the dust below it: small pools remain on the cobbles. They look like footprints; footprints she might have left herself, gleaming like mirrors. For a moment they contain her face, dark against the glare; then only the blank blue sky.

Passing through the Ghetto she pauses. Over a door, an inscription she had never noticed before, though it's been here for centuries. ID VELIS QUOD POSSIS: *I wish only for what I can have.*

She passes through a shaft of hot light, heading to the end of the street and the bus stop that will take her home.

# Acknowledgments

Writing any book, especially a book about oneself, can be a lonely and puzzling business, as well as a gleeful one. I could not have done it without the most excellent conversations, advice and encouragement of my dear friends, especially Alice Williams, Beth Norling, Toni Jordan, Ann Leander, Jon Bauer, Sharlene Miller-Brown, Cassandra Austin, Daniel McGlone, Matt Pritchard, Imogen Wood, Charlotte Gordon, Simon Tong, Mary Stacy Hoffman (who painstakingly corrected my Italian), Mandy Brett, Michael Williams, Antoni Jach, the late Laurie Clancy, Tracey Callendar, and my ever-understanding wonderful parents, Margot and Geoff. Bless you and thank you.

I would also like to thank, in absentia, all the people who appear in this book, for the lessons they taught me and for the friendship they offered.

*The Romantic* was begun in Rome, during a six-month fellowship at the B. R. Whiting Library given through the generosity of the Australia Council for the Arts. I am very grateful to Mrs Lorri Whiting for donating her apartment to the cause of writers in need of concentration and the great adventure of history, drama and beauty that is Rome.

I was also given time to work on the book at Varuna, the Writers House, thanks to Peter Bishop and the team, and the auspices of the CAL Second Book Fellowship. The house itself and the writers I have met there made that time and the work a joy.

At Text, I had the privilege of working again with Michael Heyward: *mille grazie, principe*. The incredibly diligent and patient editing of Caro Cooper, design by W. H. Chong and Susan Miller, and the help of all the crew made this book happen.

Readers of my first memoir gave me the nerve to write the second with their generous letters, comments and empathy. I am humbled by their kindness.

Finally, gratitude and admiration to Lord Byron for his wit, Percy Bysshe Shelley for his heart, Johann Wolfgang von Goethe for his delight, and Giacomo Girolamo Casanova for his daring; to Richard Holmes for his inspiring *Footsteps: Adventures of a Romantic Biographer* and *Sidetracks: Explorations of a Romantic Biographer*; and to the late Eleanor Clark for *Rome and a Villa*, which remains my favourite book about the magic of Rome. They are all unwittingly present in this small addition to the literature of that amazing city.